THE DESTINED INNOVATOR

ROHAN SHAW

Copyright © 2023 Rohan Shaw

All rights reserved.

ISBN:

This book has been self-published with all reasonable efforts taken to make the material error-free by the author. No part of this book shall be used, reproduced in any manner whatsoever without written permission from the author, except in the case of brief quotations embodied in critical articles and reviews.

The Author of this book is solely responsible and liable for its content including but not limited to the views, representations, descriptions, statements, information, opinions, and references. The Content of this book shall not constitute or be construed or deemed to reflect the opinion or expression of the Publisher or Editor. Neither the Publisher nor Editor endorse or approve the Content of this book or guarantee the reliability, accuracy or completeness of the Content published herein and do not make any representations or warranties of any kind, express or implied, including but not limited to the implied warranties of merchantability, fitness for a particular purpose. The Publisher and Editor shall not be liable whatsoever for any errors, omissions, whether such errors or omissions result from negligence, accident, or any other cause or claims for loss or damages of any kind, including without limitation, indirect or consequential loss or damage arising out of use, inability to use, or about the reliability, accuracy or sufficiency of the information contained in this book.

DEDICATION

To my family, thank you for always believing in me and supporting my dreams. Your love and guidance have been invaluable to me as I pursued my passion for innovation and creativity. This book is dedicated to you with love and gratitude.

---- Rohan Shaw

CONTENTS

Foreword vii
Preface viii
ACKNOWLEDGMENTS 1
INTRODUCTION 2
Encouraging a Culture of Innovation 7
Idea Generation Techniques 35
Evaluating and selecting ideas 57
Prototyping and Testing 79
Implementing New Ideas 104
Overcoming Barriers to Innovations 133
The Role of Leadership in Fostering Innovation ... 159
Innovation and Customer Needs 194
Bibliography 231
About The Author 232
Glossary 234

Foreword

In today's fast-paced and constantly changing business landscape, innovation and creativity are more important than ever. Companies that can adapt and come up with new ideas have a significant advantage over their competitors, and employees who can think creatively are in high demand. But fostering a culture of innovation and generating new ideas is easier said than done.

That's where this book comes in. Rohan Shaw has compiled a wealth of knowledge and practical strategies for encouraging creativity and driving innovation in the workplace. From providing resources for innovation to recognizing and rewarding employees who come up with new ideas, Rohan Shaw covers it all. Plus, with techniques like brainstorming, lateral thinking, and design thinking, you'll have a variety of methods for generating fresh ideas.

But Rohan Shaw doesn't stop there. He also provides tools for evaluating and selecting the best ideas, as well as strategies for implementing them effectively. And if you're worried about risk and uncertainty, Rohan Shaw has you covered with his tips for managing risk and building a team to execute your plan.

This book is a valuable resource for anyone looking to boost creativity and innovation in their business or organization. Whether you're an entrepreneur, a manager, or an employee, you'll find valuable insights and practical advice within these pages. So let's get started on your journey to becoming a destined innovator!"

PREFACE

When I first started writing books as a part of my hobby, I was constantly told to 'think outside the box' and 'be creative.' But as I soon discovered, it's one thing to be said to be creative, and quite another to do it. Generating new ideas and coming up with creative solutions to problems isn't always easy, and it requires a combination of skills and mindset.

Over the years, I've learned a lot about the process of innovation and creativity, and I've developed a number of strategies for encouraging and fostering a culture of innovation in the workplace. I've also experimented with a variety of techniques for generating new ideas, and I've learned what works and what doesn't.

In this book, I've compiled my insights and experiences in the hope of helping others boost their creativity and drive innovation in their businesses or organizations. Whether you're an entrepreneur, a manager, or an employee, I believe that everyone has the potential to be creative and innovative. And with the right tools and strategies, anyone can learn to think creatively and generate new ideas.

I hope that this book will serve as a valuable resource for anyone looking to tap into their creative potential and drive progress in their field. Let's get started on your journey to becoming an innovator!"

ACKNOWLEDGMENTS

I would like to express my sincere gratitude to myself for editing and publishing this book.

As the editor, I poured countless hours into refining and shaping the content of this book, ensuring that it was accurate, useful, and engaging for readers. I am grateful for the opportunity to share my knowledge and experiences with others, and I hope that this book will be a valuable resource for anyone looking to drive innovation and creativity in their business.

As the publisher, I am thankful for the opportunity to bring this book to fruition. From the initial concept to the final product, I have dedicated myself to ensuring that this book meets the highest standards of quality. I am proud to have played a role in bringing this book to the world, and I hope that it will be well-received by readers.

Finally, I want to extend my thanks to the countless experts and thought leaders who have shared their knowledge and experiences with me. Their insights and perspectives have been invaluable in helping me to understand the complexities of fostering innovation and creativity in the business world.

Thank you all for your contributions to this book. It would not have been possible without your help and support.

INTRODUCTION

Are you tired of the same old ideas and solutions at your organization? Do you want to shake things up and drive real innovation and creativity? Look no further! This book is the ultimate guide to fostering a culture of innovation in the business world.

From encouraging risk-taking and providing resources for innovation, to nurturing a growth mindset and fostering collaboration, we'll cover all the key strategies for creating an environment that encourages creativity. We'll also delve into a variety of idea-generation techniques, including brainstorming, lateral thinking, and design thinking, to help you come up with new and innovative ideas.

But it's not enough just to have good ideas - you also need to know how to evaluate and select the best ones and turn them into reality. That's why we'll cover everything from how to create a plan from implementation to managing the process and measuring the success of your ideas.

So don't miss out on this opportunity to take your organization to the next level. Start reading this book now and learn how to drive innovation and creativity in your business.

In today's fast-paced business environment innovation and creativity are most important. Companies that can consistently generate and implement new ideas have a distinct advantage over their competitors. However, fostering a culture of innovation and creativity is not always easy. It requires a united effort to create an environment that encourages employees to think outside the box and take calculated risks.

This book aims to provide a comprehensive guide to innovation and creativity in the business world. We'll cover everything from how to create a culture that fosters creativity, to a variety of techniques for generating new ideas and strategies for turning those ideas into reality. We'll also delve into how to evaluate and select the most promising ideas and how to manage the implementation process to ensure success.

Whether you're a business leader looking to drive innovation within your organization, or an individual looking to cultivate your creative skills, this book has something to offer. We'll provide practical tips and techniques that you can put into action right away, as well as case studies and examples of companies that have successfully fostered a culture of innovation. By the end of this book, you'll have a solid understanding of what it takes to drive innovation and creativity in your business.

In addition to exploring the key strategies and tactics for fostering innovation and creativity, this book will also delve into the importance of continuous learning and personal growth. We'll discuss the role that a "growth mindset" plays in encouraging employees to seek out new challenges and embrace failure as an opportunity to learn and improve. We'll also cover the importance of providing opportunities for creative expression, and how recognizing and rewarding innovative ideas can help to create a virtuous cycle of continuous improvement.

Finally, we'll delve into the challenges that can arise when implementing new ideas, and how to navigate them successfully. This includes managing the impact of change on the organization and its stakeholders, as well as tracking and measuring the success of the implemented idea.

Overall, this book provides a comprehensive guide to driving innovation and creativity in the business world. By following the strategies and tactics outlined in these pages, you'll be ready on your way to foster a culture of continuous improvement and driving your organization to new heights of success.

One of the key themes of this book is the importance of collaboration and idea-sharing in fostering a culture of innovation.

We'll discuss the benefits of creating a culture of openness and collaboration and provide tips for encouraging employees to share their ideas and work with others to develop them. This includes strategies for creating the right physical and virtual spaces for collaboration, as well as techniques for facilitating effective teamwork and idea-sharing sessions.

We'll also explore the role that diversity and inclusion play in fostering innovation. A diverse workforce brings a range of perspectives and experiences to the table, which can lead to a wider variety of ideas and solutions. We'll discuss the importance of building an inclusive culture that values and encourages the contributions of all employees, regardless of their background or characteristics.

Overall, this book provides a wealth of practical advice and strategies for creating an environment that encourages innovation and creativity.

The Destined Innovator

The Destined Innovator

ONE

Encouraging a Culture of Innovation

How to create an environment that fosters creativity and encourages employees to come up with new ideas ?

Encouraging a culture of innovation is essential for businesses that want to stay competitive and adapt to changing market conditions. Innovation allows businesses to create new products and services, improve existing ones, and find new and efficient ways of doing things. However, innovation doesn't just happen – it requires a supportive and enabling environment.

To create a culture of innovation in your organization, it's important to communicate the importance of innovation to your employees. Make it clear that innovation is a key part of your company's strategy, and that it is valued and rewarded. This will help to create a sense of purpose and encourage employees to come up with new ideas.

Encouraging a growth mindset is another important aspect of creating a culture of innovation. Encourage employees to embrace challenges, learn from mistakes, and improve continuously. This will foster a sense of resilience and encourage employees to think outside the box.

Fostering a culture of collaboration and open communication is also crucial for innovation. Encourage employees to share ideas and work together to find creative solutions. This can be achieved through things like team-building activities, cross-functional collaboration, and open communication channels.

Providing resources and support for innovation is another important aspect of creating a culture of innovation. This could include things like training, funding for innovation projects, and access to new technologies and tools. By providing employees with the resources, they need to innovate you can help them to create an enabling environment for creativity.

Encouraging risk-taking and experimentation is also key to fostering a culture of innovation. Encourage employees to try out new ideas, even if they may not work out as planned. This can be achieved through things like hackathons, innovation labs, and other initiatives that encourage experimentation.

Recognizing and rewarding innovation is another important aspect of creating a culture of innovation. Make it clear that innovation is valued and rewarded in your organization, and give credit where credit is due. This will help to create a sense of ownership and encourage employees to come up with new ideas.

Encouraging continuous learning is also crucial for fostering a culture of innovation. Encourage employees to stay up to date on industry developments and new technologies and provide opportunities for them to learn and grow. This could include things like training programs, conference attendance, and other learning opportunities.

Creating a positive and inclusive work culture is also important for fostering a culture of innovation. A positive work culture that values diversity and inclusivity can foster a sense of belonging and encourage employees to share their ideas and be more creative.

Encouraging employees to take breaks and have a healthy work-life balance can also improve creativity and productivity. Studies have shown that taking breaks and having a healthy work-life balance can improve creativity and productivity.

Encouraging employees to think outside the box is another important aspect of fostering a culture of innovation. Encourage employees to challenge assumptions and think creatively about problems and opportunities. This can be achieved through things like design thinking workshops and other initiatives that encourage out-of-the-box thinking.

Encouraging employees to seek out diverse perspectives is also crucial for fostering a culture of innovation. Encourage employees to seek out diverse perspectives, whether it be through interacting with people from different backgrounds, reading about different cultures, or learning about new industries. This can help to broaden employees' horizons and encourage them to come up with new and innovative ideas.

Fostering a culture of curiosity is another important aspect of creating a culture of innovation. Encourage employees to ask questions, seek out new knowledge, and be curious about the world around them. This can help to spark new ideas and encourage employees to think creatively.

Encouraging employees to challenge the status quo is also important for fostering a culture of innovation. Encourage employees to question the way things are currently done and look for ways to improve processes and systems. This can be achieved through initiatives like process improvement workshops and problem-solving sessions.

Providing opportunities for employees to work on passion projects is another way to foster a culture of innovation. Allowing employees to work on projects that they are passionate about can foster a sense of ownership and encourage them to come up with innovative solutions.

Encouraging employees to take on leadership roles is another way to foster a culture of innovation. Encourage employees to take on leadership roles, whether it be through leading innovation projects or taking on additional responsibilities. This can help to develop leadership skills and encourage employees to come up with new ideas.

Encouraging employees to collaborate with people outside of their team or department is also important for fostering a culture of innovation. This can help to bring new perspectives and ideas to the table and encourage cross-functional collaboration.

By implementing these strategies, businesses can create a culture of innovation that encourages employees to come up with new and creative ideas and helps the business stay competitive and adapt to changing market conditions.

Encouraging risk-taking

Strategies for creating an environment where it is safe for employees to take risks and propose new ideas.

Encouraging risk-taking is an essential aspect of fostering a culture of innovation within an organization. Without an acceptance of risk and a willingness to try new things, it can be difficult for employees to come up with and pursue new ideas. However, creating an environment where it is safe for employees to take risks and propose new ideas is not always easy. There are several strategies that leaders can use to encourage risk-taking and create a culture of innovation within their organization:

- Lead by example: As a leader, it is important to model a willingness to take risks and embrace new ideas. This can help to create a culture where it is okay for others to do the same.
- Encourage open communication: Encourage employees to speak up and share their ideas, even if they may be unconventional or risky. This can be done through open forums, suggestion boxes, or other channels.
- Support failure: It is important to create an environment where failure is viewed as a natural part of the innovation process. Encourage employees to learn from their mistakes and use them as opportunities for growth.
- Provide resources: Make sure that employees have the resources they need to pursue new ideas, including time, funding, and support.
- Encourage experimentation: Encourage employees to experiment and try new things, even if it means stepping outside of their comfort zone.
- Recognize and reward innovation: Recognize and reward employees who come up with new ideas and take risks, even if their ideas do not stand out. This can help to

create a culture of innovation.

By adopting these strategies, leaders can create an environment that is conducive to risk-taking and innovation. This can help to foster a culture of innovation within the organization and drive the adoption of new ideas and practices. Leaders need to remember that fostering a culture of innovation is a continuous process, and it requires ongoing effort and commitment. This includes regularly soliciting input and feedback from employees, staying up to date on industry trends and emerging technologies, and continuously seeking out new opportunities for innovation.

Creating an environment that encourages risk-taking and innovation can also have several benefits for the organization. It can lead to the development of new products and services that meet customer needs, drive business growth and competitiveness, and improve efficiency and productivity. By fostering a culture of innovation, leaders can create an organization that is agile and able to adapt to change and position it for long-term success in an increasingly dynamic and competitive business environment.

In addition to the strategies outlined above, there are a few additional steps that leaders can take to encourage risk-taking and innovation within their organization. These include:

- Providing training and development opportunities: By investing in the development of their employees, leaders can help to build the skills and knowledge needed to generate and pursue new ideas.
- Encouraging cross-functional collaboration: By bringing employees from different departments and functions together to work on projects, leaders can create an environment that fosters collaboration and idea-sharing.
- Creating a supportive work culture: By building a positive and supportive work culture, leaders can create an

environment where employees feel comfortable taking risks and sharing their ideas.

By adopting these strategies, leaders can create a culture that encourages risk-taking and innovation and position their organization for long-term success.

"Risk and Reward: How One Tech CEO Encouraged Innovation and Reaped the Benefits"

As the CEO of a successful tech company, Prity was starting to worry. Despite its track record of innovation, the company had recently hit a lull in new ideas. Prity knew that they needed to take risks to stay ahead in their competitive industry, but her employees seemed afraid to suggest new ideas.

Determined to shake things up, Prity decided to act. She knew that she needed to create an environment where it was safe for her employees to take risks and propose new ideas, even if they might not all succeed.

First, she made sure to lead by example. She started sharing her risky ideas with her team and encouraged them to do the same. She also implemented open communication channels, such as suggestion boxes and regular brainstorming sessions, to make it easier for employees to share their ideas.

Next, Prity made it clear that failure was a natural part of the innovation process. She encouraged her team to embrace mistakes as opportunities for growth and learning and provided resources such as training and development opportunities to help them develop new skills and knowledge.

Prity also encouraged experimentation and made it clear that it was okay to try new things, even if they were outside of an employee's comfort zone. She provided the necessary resources, such as time and funding, to help employees pursue their ideas.

Finally, Prity recognized and rewarded employees who took risks and proposed new ideas, even if they didn't all pan out. She created a culture of innovation by regularly soliciting input and feedback from her team, staying up to date on industry trends and emerging technologies, and continuously seeking out new opportunities for innovation.

As a result of these efforts, Prity's tech company saw a surge in new ideas and a renewed sense of creativity among its employees. The company was able to stay ahead of its competitors and continue to grow and thrive in its industry. Prity's efforts to create an environment that encouraged risk-taking had paid off and the company was better positioned for long-term success.

Providing resources for innovation

How to make sure that employees have the time, resources, and support they need to generate and pursue new ideas?

Providing resources for innovation is an essential aspect of fostering a culture of innovation within an organization. Without the necessary resources, it can be difficult for employees to generate and pursue new ideas. However, ensuring that employees have the time, resources, and support they need to be creative and innovative can be a challenge. Here are a few strategies that leaders can use to provide the necessary resources for innovation:

1. Allocate dedicated time for innovation: Employees need time to think, brainstorm, and explore new ideas. One way to provide this time is to allocate dedicated blocks of time for innovation, such as "innovation hours" or "idea days." This can help to ensure that employees have the time they need to focus on generating and pursuing new ideas.
2. Provide resources for experimentation: To test and refine new ideas, employees may need access to resources such as materials, equipment, or software. Providing these resources can help to facilitate experimentation and enable employees to pursue their ideas.
3. Offer training and development opportunities: Providing employees with training and development opportunities can help to build the skills and knowledge they need to generate and pursue new ideas. This can include things like workshops, training sessions, or online courses.
4. Encourage cross-functional collaboration: By bringing employees from different departments and functions together to work on projects, leaders can create an environment that fosters collaboration and idea-sharing.

This can be facilitated through regular meetings, hackathons, or other events.
5. Create a supportive work culture: Building a positive and supportive work culture can help to create an environment where employees feel comfortable taking risks and sharing their ideas. This can include things like open communication channels, recognition and reward programs, and a focus on continuous learning and improvement.

By adopting these strategies, leaders can provide the necessary resources for innovation and create an environment that is conducive to the generation and pursuit of new ideas. This can help to foster a culture of innovation within the organization and drive the adoption of new practices and technologies. Leaders need to remember that providing resources for innovation is an ongoing process, and it requires ongoing effort and commitment. This includes regularly soliciting input and feedback from employees, staying up to date on industry trends and emerging technologies, and continuously seeking out new opportunities for innovation.

"Innovation Unlimited: Empowering Employees to Turn Ideas into Reality"

As the CEO of a rapidly growing company, Nandini knew that innovation was key to maintaining a competitive edge. But despite her best efforts to encourage new ideas and foster a culture of creativity, she often struggled to get her employees fully on board. Many seemed to be too busy with their day-to-day tasks to focus on coming up with new ideas, and those that did come up with ideas often struggled to get the resources and support they needed to see them through to fruition.

Determined to find a solution, Nandini began to research the best practices for fostering innovation within an organization. She learned about the importance of providing dedicated time and resources for innovation, as well as the value of inclusive decision-making and a supportive environment that promoted creativity.

Armed with this knowledge, Nandini set out to implement a series of changes within her company. She established dedicated innovation days, during which employees were encouraged to set aside their regular tasks and focus on coming up with new ideas. She also established an innovation fund, which provided financial support for employees who had promising ideas but needed additional resources to bring them to life. And she made a point of recognizing and rewarding employees who made significant contributions to the innovation process.

The results were nothing short of astounding. With the time, resources, and support they needed to pursue their ideas, Nandini's employees began to come up with all sorts of innovative solutions to the challenges facing the company. And as these solutions were implemented, the company saw significant improvements in efficiency, customer satisfaction, and overall performance.

Thanks to Nandini's efforts, the company's culture of innovation had truly taken root, and it showed in every aspect of the business. And with her practical guide to cultivating a culture of innovation, Nandini was able to share her success with other leaders looking to drive innovation within their organizations.

Encouraging experimentation and failure

How to embrace failure as a natural part of the innovation process?

As a business leader, you know that innovation is crucial to the success of your organization. But all too often, the fear of failure can hold employees back from taking risks and trying new things. In this short book, we'll explore the importance of encouraging experimentation and embracing failure as a natural part of the innovation process.

First, it's important to understand that failure is not the opposite of success – it's an essential part of the journey. Every time we fail, we have the opportunity to learn and grow. By encouraging employees to view failure as a learning opportunity rather than a setback, you create a culture of experimentation that is more likely to lead to breakthrough innovations.

So how can you foster this culture of experimentation within your organization? Here are a few strategies to consider:

1. Create a safe space for failure: Make it clear to employees that it's okay to take risks and try new things, even if they don't always work out. Encourage a culture of transparency and honesty, where it's safe to admit when something isn't working and where it's okay to ask for help.
2. Encourage a growth mindset: Rather than viewing failure as a personal flaw, encourage employees to see it as an opportunity to learn and grow. Help them develop a growth mindset, where they see challenges as a chance to improve and become more resilient.

3. Provide support and resources: Make sure that employees have the resources and support they need to take risks and try new things. This might include dedicated time for experimentation, access to training and development opportunities, or financial support for new projects.

By embracing failure and encouraging experimentation, you'll create a culture of innovation that is more likely to lead to success in the long run. So don't be afraid to take risks and encourage your employees to do the same – you never know where it might lead!

"The Failure Factor: How Embracing Mistakes Leads to Success"

As the CEO of a rapidly growing tech company, Ayush knew that innovation was key to staying ahead of the competition. But despite his efforts to foster a culture of creativity and encourage his employees to take risks, he found that many of them were still hesitant to try new things. They were afraid of making mistakes and failing, and as a result, they were often reluctant to take on new challenges.

Determined to find a way to break through this fear of failure, Ayush began to research the best practices for encouraging experimentation and embracing mistakes as a natural part of the innovation process. He learned about the importance of creating a safe space for failure, encouraging a growth mindset, and providing support and resources for employees who wanted to take risks and try new things.

Armed with this knowledge, Ayush set out to implement a series of changes within his company. He established dedicated innovation days, during which employees were encouraged to set aside their regular tasks and focus on coming up with new ideas. He also established an innovation fund, which provided financial support for employees who had promising ideas but needed additional resources to bring them to life. And he made a point of recognizing and rewarding employees who made significant contributions to the innovation process, even if their ideas didn't always work out.

With the time, resources, and support they needed to pursue their ideas, Ayush's employees began to come up with all sorts of innovative solutions to the challenges facing the company. And as these solutions were implemented, the company saw significant improvements in efficiency, customer satisfaction, and overall performance.

Thanks to Ayush's efforts, the company's culture of innovation had truly taken root, and it showed in every aspect of the business. And with his practical guide to embracing failure and encouraging experimentation, Ayush was able to share his success with other leaders looking to drive innovation within their own organizations.

Nurturing a growth mindset

Strategies for helping employees develop a "growth mindset" and a belief in their own ability to learn and grow.

As a business leader, you know that success is often driven by the ability to adapt and learn in the face of changing circumstances. But how do you foster a culture of continuous learning and improvement within your organization? One key strategy is to nurture a growth mindset among your employees.

But what exactly is a growth mindset? According to Stanford University psychologist Carol Dweck, a growth mindset is the belief that one's abilities and intelligence can be developed through effort, learning, and practice. In contrast, a fixed mindset is the belief that one's abilities and intelligence are fixed and cannot be changed.

Research has shown that those with a growth mindset are more likely to embrace challenges, persist in the face of setbacks, and learn from their mistakes. This is because they believe that their abilities can be improved through effort, rather than viewing failures as a sign of inherent limitations.

So how can you nurture a growth mindset within your organization? Here are a few strategies to consider:

1. Encourage a culture of continuous learning: Make it clear to employees that learning, and growth are valued and encouraged within your organization. Offer opportunities for training and development, and create a supportive environment where employees feel comfortable asking questions and seeking out new challenges.
2. Model a growth mindset: As a leader, your mindset sets the tone for your organization. By demonstrating a

willingness to learn and grow yourself, you can encourage others to do the same.
3. Recognize and reward effort and progress: Rather than just focusing on end results, make a point of recognizing and rewarding employees for their hard work and progress. This helps to reinforce the idea that learning, and growth are valued within your organization.

By nurturing a growth mindset within your organization, you'll create a culture of continuous learning and improvement that is more likely to lead to success in the long run. So don't be afraid to embrace challenges and encourage your employees to do the same – you never know where it might lead!

"The Growth Mindset Revolution: Transforming Your Business through Continuous Learning and Improvement"

As the CEO of a rapidly growing company, Eliza knew that success was all about adapting and evolving in the face of change. But despite her efforts to encourage a culture of continuous learning and improvement, she found that many of her employees were stuck in a fixed mindset, viewing their abilities and intelligence as fixed and unchanging.

Determined to find a way to shift this mindset, Eliza began to research the concept of a growth mindset and its importance for business success. She learned about the importance of cultivating a belief in one's own ability to learn and grow, and the value of embracing challenges and persisting in the face of setbacks.

Armed with this knowledge, Eliza set out to implement a series of changes within her company. She established a culture of continuous learning, offering regular training and development opportunities for employees and encouraging them to seek out new challenges. She also made a point of recognizing and rewarding effort and progress, rather than just focusing on end results.

As employees began to adopt a growth mindset, they became more open to learning and more willing to take on new challenges. And as a result, the company saw significant improvements in efficiency, productivity, and overall performance.

Eliza was able to share her success with other leaders looking to transform their businesses through continuous learning and improvement

Fostering collaboration and idea sharing

Tips for creating a culture of openness and collaboration.

As a business leader, you know that collaboration is key to driving innovation and solving complex problems. But how do you create a culture of openness and collaboration within your organization? In this short book, we'll explore the importance of fostering collaboration and idea-sharing and offer practical tips for building a culture that encourages these practices.

First, it's important to understand the value of collaboration. When employees feel comfortable sharing their ideas and working with others to develop them, they are more likely to come up with creative solutions and more efficient ways of working. Collaboration also helps to build trust and foster a sense of community within an organization, which can lead to increased job satisfaction and retention.

So how can you foster collaboration and idea-sharing within your organization? Here are a few strategies to consider:

- Encourage open communication: Make it clear to employees that their ideas and input are valued. Encourage open and honest communication and create a culture where it's safe to share ideas and ask questions.

- Encourage teamwork: Encourage employees to work together in cross-functional teams or on collaborative projects. This can help to break down silos and foster a sense of community within your organization.

- Recognize and reward collaboration: Make a point of

recognizing and rewarding employees who contribute to a culture of collaboration and idea-sharing. This can help to reinforce the importance of these practices within your organization.

By fostering collaboration and idea-sharing, you'll create a culture of openness and creativity that is more likely to lead to success in the long run. So don't be afraid to encourage your employees to share their ideas and work together.

"Collaboration Works: Building a Culture of Openness and Idea Sharing"

As the CEO of a rapidly growing company, Rachel knew that collaboration was key to driving innovation and solving complex problems. But despite her efforts to encourage a culture of openness and collaboration, she found that many of her employees were hesitant to share their ideas and work with others. They seemed to be stuck in a "silo mentality," focused on their tasks and goals rather than working together as a team.

Determined to find a way to break through this barrier, Rachel began to research the best practices for fostering collaboration and idea sharing within an organization. She learned about the value of open communication, teamwork, and recognizing and rewarding collaboration.

She encouraged open and honest communication and made a point of recognizing and rewarding employees who contributed to a culture of collaboration and idea sharing. She also established cross-functional teams and encouraged employees to work together on collaborative projects.

With the encouragement and support they needed to share their ideas and work together; Rachel's employees began to come up with all sorts of innovative solutions to the challenges facing the company. And as these solutions were implemented, the company saw significant improvements in efficiency, productivity, and overall performance.

Thanks to Rachel's efforts, the company's culture of collaboration and idea sharing had truly taken root, and it showed in every aspect of the business. And with her practical guide to building a culture of openness and collaboration, Rachel was able to share her success with other leaders looking to drive innovation within their own organizations.

Encouraging continuous learning

How to create a culture of continuous learning, where employees are encouraged to seek out new skills?

As a business leader, you know that success is often driven by the ability to adapt and learn in the face of changing circumstances. But how do you create a culture of continuous learning within your organization? One key strategy is to encourage employees to seek out new knowledge and skills that can help them generate innovative ideas.

But how do you do this? Here are a few strategies to consider:

- Encourage a culture of continuous learning: Make it clear to employees that learning and growth are valued and encouraged within your organization. Offer opportunities for training and development, and create a supportive environment where employees feel comfortable asking questions and seeking out new challenges.

- Foster a culture of curiosity: Encourage employees to be curious and to ask questions about their work and the industry. This can help stimulate creativity and drive innovation.

- Provide access to resources and tools: Make sure that employees have access to the resources and tools they need to learn and grow. This might include access to industry publications, training courses, or online learning platforms.

By fostering a culture of continuous learning, you'll create an environment that is more conducive to innovation and adaptability.

"The Endless Learning Curve: How to Foster a Culture of Continuous Improvement and Innovation"

As the CEO of a rapidly growing company, Sergio knew that success was all about adapting and evolving in the face of change. But despite his efforts to encourage a culture of continuous learning and improvement, he found that many of his employees were stuck in their ways, unwilling to seek out new knowledge and skills.

Determined to find a way to shift this mindset, Sergio began to research the best practices for fostering a culture of continuous learning within an organization. He learned about the importance of creating a supportive environment that encouraged employees to be curious and seek out new challenges, as well as the value of providing access to resources and tools that could help them learn and grow.

Armed with this knowledge, Sergio set out to implement a series of changes within his company. He established a culture of continuous learning, offering regular training and development opportunities for employees and encouraging them to seek out new challenges. He also made a point of recognizing and rewarding effort and progress, rather than just focusing on results.

The results were nothing short of astounding. As employees began to embrace a culture of continuous learning, they became more open to new ideas and more willing to take on new challenges. And as a result, the company saw significant improvements in efficiency, productivity, and overall performance.

Thanks to Sergio's efforts, the company's culture of continuous learning and improvement had truly taken root, and it showed in every aspect of the business. And with his practical guide to fostering a culture of continuous learning, Sergio was able to share his success with other leaders looking to drive innovation within their organizations.

Providing opportunities for creative expression

Ways to encourage employees to express themselves creatively and think outside the box.

As a business leader, you know that creativity is crucial to driving innovation and staying ahead of the competition. But how do you encourage your employees to think outside the box and express themselves creatively? Here are a few strategies to consider:

- Provide opportunities for creative expression: Encourage employees to take breaks from their regular tasks and engage in activities that allow them to express themselves creatively. This might include things like art or music classes, writing workshops, or other activities that allow them to tap into their creative side.

- Foster a culture of openness and inclusivity: Create an environment where employees feel comfortable sharing their ideas and expressing themselves freely. This might involve things like inclusive decision-making processes, open-door policies, or regular opportunities for employees to share their thoughts and ideas.

- Recognize and reward creative thinking: Make a point of recognizing and rewarding employees who come up with innovative ideas or think creatively. This helps to reinforce the idea that creativity is valued within your organization.

By providing opportunities for creative expression and fostering a culture of openness and inclusivity, you'll create an environment that is more conducive to innovation and creative thinking. So don't be afraid to encourage your employees to think outside the box.

"The Creative Spark: How to Ignite Innovation and Encourage Out-of-the-Box Thinking"

As the CEO of a rapidly growing company, Tokyo knew that creativity was key to staying ahead of the competition. But despite her efforts to foster a culture of innovation, she found that many of her employees were stuck in a rut, unwilling to think outside the box and express themselves creatively.

Determined to find a way to spark their creative juices, Tokyo began to research the best practices for encouraging creative expression within an organization. She learned about the importance of providing opportunities for creative expression and fostering a culture of openness and inclusivity.

Armed with this knowledge, Tokyo set out to implement a series of changes within her company. She established regular breaks for creative expression, offering art and music classes and writing workshops for employees to tap into their creative side. She also made a point of recognizing and rewarding employees who came up with innovative ideas or thought creatively.

The results were nothing short of astounding. As employees began to embrace a culture of creativity and innovation, they became more open to new ideas and more willing to take on new challenges. And as a result, the company saw significant improvements in efficiency, productivity, and overall performance.

With her practical guide to encouraging creative expression, Tokyo was able to share her success with other leaders looking to drive innovation within their own organizations.

Recognizing and rewarding

innovation

Strategies for recognizing and rewarding employees who come up with new ideas and contribute to the company.

As a business leader, you know that innovation is key to driving success and staying ahead of the competition. But how do you encourage your employees to come up with new ideas and contribute to your company's culture of innovation? One key strategy is to recognize and reward their efforts.

But how do you do this effectively? Here are a few strategies to consider:

- Make it clear that innovation is valued: Make it clear to your employees that innovation is valued within your organization. This might involve things like regularly communicating the importance of innovation, setting clear goals and objectives related to innovation, and recognizing and rewarding employees who make significant contributions to the innovation process.

- Create a rewards program: Consider establishing a rewards program that specifically recognizes and rewards employees who come up with new ideas or contribute to the company's culture of innovation. This could involve things like financial bonuses, recognition at company-wide meetings, or other forms of recognition.

- Provide resources and support: In order to encourage innovation, you'll need to provide your employees with the resources and support they need to bring their ideas to life. This might involve things like dedicated innovation days, an innovation fund, or access to resources and tools that can help them develop and test their ideas.

By recognizing and rewarding innovation, you'll create a culture that encourages your employees to think creatively and come up with new ideas that can drive your company's success. So don't be afraid to show your appreciation for their efforts – it can go a long way in driving innovation within your organization.

"The Innovation Factor: How Recognizing and Rewarding Employees Can Drive Success"

As the CEO of a rapidly growing company, John knew that innovation was key to staying ahead of the competition. But despite his efforts to foster a culture of innovation, he found that many of his employees were hesitant to come forward with new ideas, fearing that they wouldn't be recognized or rewarded for their efforts.

Determined to find a way to change this mindset, John began to research the best practices for recognizing and rewarding innovation within an organization. He learned about the importance of making it clear that innovation is valued, establishing rewards programs that specifically recognize and reward innovative ideas, and providing resources and support to help employees bring their ideas to life.

Armed with this knowledge, John set out to implement a series of changes within his company. He established a rewards program that specifically recognized and rewarded employees who came up with new ideas or contributed to the company's culture of innovation. He also provided dedicated innovation days, an innovation fund, and access to resources and tools to help employees develop and test their ideas.

The results were nothing short of astounding. As employees began to feel recognized and rewarded for their innovative efforts, they became more willing to come forward with new ideas and more engaged in the innovation process. And as a result, the company saw significant improvements in efficiency, productivity, and overall performance.

TWO

IDEA GENERATION TECHNIQUES

A variety of methods for generating new ideas such as brainstorming, lateral thinking, and design thinking.

Idea generation is a crucial step in the innovation process, as it involves coming up with new and creative ideas that can be developed into products or services. There are a variety of techniques that businesses can use to generate new ideas, including brainstorming, lateral thinking, and design thinking.

Brainstorming is a widely used technique for generating new ideas. It involves bringing together a group of people and encouraging them to come up with as many ideas as possible in a short period of time. The goal is to generate a large number of ideas, without worrying about the feasibility or quality of the ideas at this stage.

Lateral thinking is another technique that can be used to generate new ideas. It involves thinking about problems and opportunities in a creative and unconventional way and looking for solutions that are outside the box. Lateral thinking techniques include things like asking "what if" questions, looking for patterns and connections, and using random stimuli to spark new ideas.

Design thinking is another technique that can be used to generate new ideas. It involves a systematic and human-centred approach to problem-solving and involves identifying the needs of the user and coming up with creative solutions that meet those needs. Design thinking involves a series of steps, including empathy, definition, ideation, prototyping, and testing.

By using techniques like brainstorming, lateral thinking, and design thinking, businesses can generate a large number of ideas and identify the most promising ones to pursue

Brainstorming

The basics of brainstorming and how to run a successful brainstorming session.

Brainstorming is a creative thinking technique that involves generating as many ideas as possible without censoring or evaluating them. The goal of brainstorming is to come up with new and innovative solutions to a problem or challenge, and it can be a valuable tool for teams and individuals alike. Here are the basics of brainstorming and how to run a successful brainstorming session:

- Define the problem or challenge. Before you begin brainstorming, it's important to clearly define the problem or challenge that you are trying to solve. This will help focus your thinking and ensure that all ideas generated during the brainstorming session are relevant and useful.

- Gather a diverse group of people. Brainstorming is most effective when it involves a diverse group of people with different backgrounds, experiences, and perspectives. This can help bring new and fresh ideas to the table that may not have been considered otherwise.

- Encourage wild and crazy ideas. During the brainstorming process, it's important to encourage participants to come up with as many ideas as possible, no matter how wild or crazy they may seem. Don't worry about evaluating or censoring ideas at this stage – the goal is simply to generate as many ideas as possible.

- Use visual aids. Visual aids, such as whiteboards, post-it notes, or mind maps, can be helpful in organizing and capturing ideas during a brainstorming session. They can also help stimulate creativity and encourage participants to think in new and innovative ways.

- Don't worry about criticism. It's important to create a safe and supportive environment during a brainstorming session where participants feel free to share their ideas without fear of criticism. Encourage participants to build upon each other's ideas and to offer constructive feedback rather than criticism.

- Take breaks. Brainstorming can be mentally exhausting, so it's important to take breaks to recharge and refocus. Short breaks every 30-60 minutes can help keep participants energized and engaged.

- Evaluate and select the best ideas. Once the brainstorming session is complete, it's time to evaluate and select the best ideas. This can be done through a variety of methods, such as voting, ranking, or using a criteria-based decision-making process.

By following these steps, you can run a successful brainstorming session that generates innovative and creative ideas that can help solve problems and challenges.

"The Brainstorming Revolution: Transforming Your Business with Creative Thinking"

As the CEO of a growing tech company, Tulip was always on the lookout for new and innovative ways to stay ahead of the competition. But despite her best efforts, she found herself struggling to come up with fresh ideas that would set her company apart. That's when Tulip discovered the power of brainstorming.

By following the principles outlined in "The Brainstorming

Revolution," Tulip was able to tap into the full potential of her team's creativity and generate a steady stream of innovative ideas. She learned how to define the problem or challenge, gather a diverse group of people, encourage wild and crazy ideas, and use visual aids to stimulate creativity.

With the help of this practical guide, Tulip was able to revolutionize the way her team approached problem-solving and drive her business to new heights of success.

Whether you're a business owner, leader, or team member, "The Brainstorming Revolution" will teach you the skills you need to unleash your full creative potential and transform your business with innovative thinking.

Lateral thinking

An overview of lateral thinking and how to use it to come up with creative solutions to problems.

Lateral thinking is a creative problem-solving approach that involves looking at problems from different angles and considering unconventional solutions. The goal of lateral thinking is to generate new and innovative ideas that can help solve problems in creative and effective ways. Here is an overview of lateral thinking and how to use it to come up with creative solutions to problems:

- Define the problem or challenge. The first step in using lateral thinking to solve a problem is to clearly define the problem or challenge that you are trying to overcome. This will help focus your thinking and ensure that you are considering solutions that are relevant and useful.

- Look at the problem from different perspectives. One of the key principles of lateral thinking is to consider problems from multiple viewpoints. This can help you see the problem in a new light and generate ideas that may not have occurred to you otherwise.

- Consider unconventional solutions. Lateral thinking involves considering solutions that may not be immediately obvious or traditional. This can help you come up with creative and innovative ideas that may not have been considered otherwise.

- Use techniques to stimulate creativity. There are a variety of techniques that you can use to stimulate creativity and help you think more laterally. These techniques include brainstorming, mind mapping, and asking "what if" questions.

- Evaluate and select the best ideas. Once you have generated a list of potential solutions, it's important to evaluate and select the best ideas. This can be done through a variety of methods, such as voting, ranking, or using a criteria-based decision-making process.

By following these steps, you can use lateral thinking to come up with creative and innovative solutions to a wide range of problems. Whether you're a business owner, leader, or individual, lateral thinking can help you think outside the box and come up with solutions that are truly unique and effective.

"The Lateral Thinker's Handbook: Creative Problem-Solving for the 21st Century"

As the CEO of a marketing firm, Raj was always on the lookout for new and innovative ways to solve his clients' problems. But despite his best efforts, he found himself stuck in a rut, coming up with the same old solutions to the same old problems. That's when Raj discovered the power of lateral thinking.

Through the techniques outlined in "The Lateral Thinker's Handbook," Raj learned how to approach problems from different angles and consider unconventional solutions. He learned how to define problems clearly, look at them from different perspectives, and use techniques like brainstorming and mind mapping to stimulate creativity.

With the help of this practical guide, Raj was able to transform the way he and his team approached problem-solving, leading to a surge of creative and innovative ideas that helped his clients stand out in their markets.

Design thinking

An introduction to design thinking and how to use it to generate and develop new ideas.

Design thinking is a creative approach to problem-solving that involves empathy, experimentation, and prototyping. It is often used to generate and develop new ideas in a variety of fields, including product design, service design, and business strategy. Here is an introduction to design thinking and how to use it to generate and develop new ideas:

- Define the problem or challenge. The first step in using design thinking to generate new ideas is to clearly define the problem or challenge that you are trying to solve. This will help focus your thinking and ensure that you are considering solutions that are relevant and useful.

- Empathize with the user. One of the key principles of design thinking is empathy – the ability to understand and share the feelings of others. When generating new ideas, it's important to consider the needs and perspectives of the user or customer. This can help you come up with ideas that are more tailored to their needs and more likely to be successful.

- Experiment and prototype. Another key principle of design thinking is experimentation – the willingness to try out new ideas and see what works. This can be done through prototyping or the creation of physical or digital models of your ideas. Prototyping allows you to test and refine your ideas in a low-risk way, helping you to identify and address any potential issues before moving forward.

- Iterate and refine. The design thinking process is not a

linear one – it involves continuous iteration and refinement of ideas as you learn and gathers more information. As you experiment and prototype, be sure to gather feedback from users and stakeholders and use it to refine and improve your ideas.

By following these steps, you can use design thinking to generate and develop new ideas that are grounded in empathy and focused on meeting the needs of the user. Whether you're a product designer, service designer, or business strategist, design thinking can help you come up with creative and innovative solutions that are both functional and desirable.

"Design Thinking for Business: Innovating for Success"

As the CEO of a rapidly growing retail company, Kylie was always on the lookout for new and innovative ways to delight her customers and stay ahead of the competition. But despite her best efforts, she found herself struggling to come up with fresh ideas that would set her company apart. That's when Kylie discovered the power of design thinking.

Through the techniques outlined in "Design Thinking for Business," Kylie learned how to approach problem-solving with empathy, experimentation, and prototyping. She learned how to define problems clearly, consider the needs and perspectives of her customers, and experiment with prototypes to test and refine her ideas.

With the help of this practical guide, Kylie was able to transform the way she and her team approached product development, leading to a surge of creative and innovative ideas that helped her company stand out in a crowded market.

SCAMPER

A technique for generating new ideas by considering different ways to modify, combine, adapt, put to other uses, eliminate or rearrange ideas.

SCAMPER is a creative thinking technique that can be used to generate new ideas by considering different ways to modify, combine, adapt, put to other uses, eliminate, rearrange, or reverse existing products, processes, or ideas. It is a useful tool for individuals and teams looking to come up with new and innovative solutions to problems or challenges. Here is an overview of SCAMPER and how to use it to generate new ideas:

- Define the problem or challenge. The first step in using SCAMPER to generate new ideas is to clearly define the problem or challenge that you are trying to solve. This will help focus your thinking and ensure that you are considering solutions that are relevant and useful.

- Consider the different elements of SCAMPER. SCAMPER stands for Substitute, Combine, Adapt, Modify, put to other uses, Eliminate, Rearrange, and Reverse. These elements can be used as prompts to stimulate creative thinking and generate new ideas.

- Substitute: Consider what you could substitute to make the product, process, or idea better. For example, you could substitute a cheaper material for a more expensive one, or a new technology for an outdated one.

- Combine: Think about what you could combine with the existing product, process, or idea to create something new and innovative. For example, you could combine two seemingly unrelated products or ideas to create a new solution.

- Adapt: Consider how you could adapt the existing product, process, or idea to meet the needs of a new market or audience.

- Modify: Think about what you could change or alter about the existing product, process, or idea to make it better.

- Put to other uses: Consider how you could use the existing product, process, or idea in a new or different way.

- Eliminate: Think about what you could remove or eliminate from the existing product, process, or idea to make it simpler or more efficient.

- Rearrange: Consider how you could rearrange the existing product, process, or idea to create something new.

- Reverse: Think about how you could reverse the existing product, process, or idea to create a new solution.

By considering these different elements of SCAMPER, you can generate a wide range of new and innovative ideas that can help solve problems or challenges in creative and effective ways. Whether you're an individual or part of a team, SCAMPER can be a valuable tool for stimulating creativity and driving innovation.

"SCAMPER Your Way to Success: A Practical Guide to Generating Innovative Ideas"

As the owner of a small design firm, Jennie was always on the lookout for new and innovative ways to stand out in a competitive market. But despite her best efforts, she found herself struggling to come up with fresh ideas that would set her company apart. That's when Jennie discovered the power of SCAMPER.

Through the techniques outlined in "SCAMPER Your Way to Success," Jennie learned how to generate new ideas by considering different ways to modify, combine, adapt, put to other uses, eliminate, rearrange, and reverse existing products, processes, and ideas. She learned how to define problems clearly and use SCAMPER as a tool to stimulate creativity and generate a wide range of innovative ideas.

With the help of this practical guide, Jennie was able to transform the way she and her team approached problem-solving, leading to a surge of creative and innovative ideas that helped her company stand out in a crowded market.

Whether you're a business owner, leader, or individual looking to boost your innovation skills, "SCAMPER Your Way to Success" is the ultimate resource for using SCAMPER to generate new and innovative ideas for your business

Reverse brainstorming

A technique for generating new ideas by starting with the desired result and working backward to identify the steps needed.

Whether you're a business owner, leader, or individual looking to boost your innovation skills, "The Reverse Brainstorming Method" is the ultimate resource for using reverse brainstorming to achieve success through creative problem-solving.

Reverse brainstorming is a creative problem-solving technique that involves starting with the desired result and working backward to identify the steps needed to achieve it. It can be a powerful tool for generating new and innovative ideas, especially when traditional brainstorming techniques have failed. Here is an overview of reverse brainstorming and how to use it to generate new ideas:

- Define the desired result. The first step in using reverse brainstorming to generate new ideas is to clearly define the result that you are trying to achieve. This will help focus your thinking and ensure that you are considering solutions that are relevant and useful.

- Work backward to identify the steps needed to achieve the result. Once you have defined the desired result, the next step is to work backward to identify the steps that are needed to achieve it. This can help you generate a range of new and innovative ideas that can help you reach your goal.

- Consider different approaches. As you work backwards to identify the steps needed to achieve the desired result, it's important to consider a range of different approaches and approaches. This can help you come up with new and innovative ideas that may not have occurred to you otherwise.

- Evaluate and select the best ideas. Once you have generated a list of potential solutions, it's important to evaluate and select the best ideas. This can be done through a variety of methods, such as voting, ranking, or using a criteria-based decision-making process.

- Implement and test your ideas. The final step in the reverse brainstorming process is to implement and test your ideas. This can be done through prototyping or other forms of experimentation, allowing you to refine and improve your ideas as you go.

By following these steps, you can use reverse brainstorming to generate new and innovative ideas that are focused on achieving a specific result. Whether you're an individual or part of a team, reverse brainstorming can be a valuable tool for stimulating creativity and driving innovation.

"The Reverse Brainstorming Method: A Practical Guide for Achieving Success through Creative Problem-Solving"

As the CEO of a fast-growing startup, Michael was always on the lookout for new and innovative ways to drive success and growth. But despite his best efforts, he found himself struggling to come up with fresh ideas that would set his company apart. That's when Michael discovered the power of reverse brainstorming.

Through the techniques outlined in "The Reverse Brainstorming Method," Michael learned how to generate new ideas by starting with the desired result and working backwards to identify the steps needed to achieve it. He learned how to define problems clearly and use reverse brainstorming as a tool to stimulate creativity and generate a wide range of innovative ideas.

With the help of this practical guide, Michael was able to transform the way he and his team approached problem-solving, leading to a surge of creative and innovative ideas that helped his company stand out in a crowded market.

The "What If?" method

A technique for generating new ideas by asking "what if?" questions and considering different scenarios.

Whether you're a business owner, leader, or individual looking to boost your innovation skills, "The Power of What If" is the ultimate resource for using scenario planning to generate new and innovative ideas.

The "What If?" method is a creative problem-solving technique that involves asking "what if?" questions and considering different scenarios. It can be a powerful tool for generating new and innovative ideas, especially when traditional brainstorming techniques have failed. Here is an overview of the "What If?" method and how to use it to generate new ideas:

- Define the problem or challenge. The first step in using the "What If?" method to generate new ideas is to clearly define the problem or challenge that you are trying to solve. This will help focus your thinking and ensure that you are considering solutions that are relevant and useful.

- Ask "what if?" questions. The key to using the "What If?" method is to ask a series of "what if?" questions that explore different scenarios and possibilities. These questions can help stimulate creativity and generate a range of new and innovative ideas.

- Consider different scenarios. As you ask, "what if?" questions and consider different scenarios, it's important to think about a range of different possibilities. This can help you come up with new and innovative ideas that may not have occurred to you otherwise.

- Evaluate and select the best ideas. Once you have generated a list of potential solutions, it's important to evaluate and select the best ideas. This can be done through a variety of methods, such as voting, ranking, or using a criteria-based decision-making process.

- Implement and test your ideas. The final step in the "What If?" method is to implement and test your ideas. This can be done through prototyping or other forms of experimentation, allowing you to refine and improve your ideas as you go.

By following these steps, you can use the "What If?" method to generate new and innovative ideas through scenario planning. Whether you're an individual or part of a team, the "What If?" method can be a valuable tool for stimulating creativity and driving innovation.

"The Power of What If : A Practical Guide to Generating Innovative Ideas through Scenario Planning"

As the CEO of a tech startup, Julie was always on the lookout for new and innovative ways to stay ahead of the competition. But despite her best efforts, she found herself struggling to come up with fresh ideas that would set her company apart. That's when Julie discovered the power of the "What If?" method.

Through the techniques outlined in "The Power of What If," Julie learned how to generate new ideas by asking "what if?" questions and considering different scenarios. She learned how to define problems clearly and use the "What If?" method as a tool to stimulate creativity and generate a wide range of innovative ideas.

With the help of this practical guide, Julie was able to transform the way she and her team approached problem-solving, leading to a surge of creative and innovative ideas that helped her company stay ahead of the curve in a rapidly changing market

Random input

A technique for generating new ideas by using random words or images as inspiration.

Whether you're a business owner, leader, or individual looking to boost your innovation skills, "The Creative Spark" is the ultimate resource for using random input to generate new and innovative ideas.

Random input is a creative problem-solving technique that involves using random words or images as inspiration. It can be a powerful tool for generating new and innovative ideas, especially when traditional brainstorming techniques have failed. Here is an overview of random input and how to use it to generate new ideas:

- Gather a list of random words or images. The first step in using random input to generate new ideas is to gather a list of random words or images that can be used as inspiration. This can be done through a variety of methods, such as using a random word generator or collecting images from magazines or the internet

- Use the words or images as inspiration. Once you have a list of random words or images, the next step is to use them as inspiration for generating new ideas. This can be done through a variety of methods, such as brainstorming, freewriting, or drawing connections between the words or images and the problem or challenge you are trying to solve.

- Evaluate and select the best ideas. Once you have generated a list of potential solutions, it's important to evaluate and select the best ideas. This can be done through a variety of methods, such as voting, ranking, or using a criteria-based decision-making process.

- Implement and test your ideas. The final step in the random input process is to implement and test your ideas. This can be done through prototyping or other forms of experimentation, allowing you to refine and improve your ideas as you go.

By following these steps, you can use random input to generate new and innovative ideas through a process of inspiration and creativity. Whether you're an individual or part of a team, random input can be a valuable tool for stimulating creativity and driving innovation.

"The Creative Spark: A Practical Guide to Generating Innovative Ideas through Random Input"

As the CEO of a creative agency, Daniel was always on the lookout for new and innovative ways to inspire his team and drive success. But despite his best efforts, he found himself struggling to come up with fresh ideas that would set his company apart. That's when Daniel discovered the power of random input.

Through the techniques outlined in "The Creative Spark," Daniel learned how to generate new ideas by using random words or images as inspiration. He learned how to use random input as a tool to stimulate creativity and generate a wide range of innovative ideas.

With the help of this practical guide, Daniel was able to transform the way he and his team approached problem-solving, leading to a surge of creative and innovative ideas that helped his company stand out in a crowded market.

The "Crazy Eights" method

A technique for generating new ideas by coming up

with eight ideas in a short amount of time.

Whether you're a business owner, leader, or individual looking to boost your innovation skills, "The Crazy Eights Method" is the ultimate resource for using the "Crazy Eights" method to generate new and innovative ideas in record time.

The "Crazy Eights" method is a creative problem-solving technique that involves coming up with eight ideas in a short amount of time. It can be a powerful tool for generating new and innovative ideas, especially when traditional brainstorming techniques have failed. Here is an overview of the "Crazy Eights" method and how to use it to generate new ideas:

- Define the problem or challenge. The first step in using the "Crazy Eights" method to generate new ideas is to clearly define the problem or challenge that you are trying to solve. This will help focus your thinking and ensure that you are considering solutions that are relevant and useful.

- Set a timer for eight minutes. The key to using the "Crazy Eights" method is to come up with eight ideas in a short amount of time. To do this, set a timer for eight minutes and use this time to generate as many ideas as possible.

- Write down as many ideas as possible. As the timer counts down, write down as many ideas as possible. Don't worry about evaluating or filtering the ideas at this stage – just focus on coming up with as many ideas as you can.

- Evaluate and select the best ideas. Once the timer has finished, review the list of ideas and evaluate them based on their feasibility, potential impact, and alignment with your goals. Select the best ideas for further development.

- Implement and test your ideas. The final step in the "Crazy Eights" process is to implement and test your ideas. This can be done through prototyping or other forms of experimentation, allowing you to refine and improve your ideas as you go.

By following these steps, you can use the "Crazy Eights" method to generate new and innovative ideas in a short amount of time. Whether you're an individual or part of a team, the "Crazy Eights" method can be a valuable tool for stimulating creativity and driving innovation.

"The Crazy Eights Method: A Practical Guide to Generating Innovative Ideas in Record Time"

As the CEO of a growing startup, Mary was always on the lookout for new and innovative ways to drive success and growth. But despite her best efforts, she found herself struggling to come up with fresh ideas that would set her company apart. That's when Mary discovered the power of the "Crazy Eights" method.

Through the techniques outlined in "The Crazy Eights Method," Mary learned how to generate new ideas by coming up with eight ideas in a short amount of time. She learned how to define problems clearly and use the "Crazy Eights" method as a tool to stimulate creativity and generate a wide range of innovative ideas.

With the help of this practical guide, Mary was able to transform the way she and her team approached problem-solving, leading to a surge of creative and innovative ideas that helped her company stand out in a crowded market.

THREE

Evaluating and selecting ideas

How to assess the potential of different ideas and choose the ones with the most promise?

Evaluating and selecting ideas is an important step in the innovation process, as it involves assessing the potential of different ideas and choosing the ones with the most promise. There are a variety of factors that businesses can consider when evaluating and selecting ideas, including feasibility, customer needs, market demand, and competitive advantage.

Feasibility is an important factor to consider when evaluating ideas. This includes looking at things like the resources and expertise required to bring the idea to fruition, as well as the potential risks and challenges.

Customer needs are also an important factor to consider when evaluating ideas. It's important to understand the needs and preferences of your target market and to ensure that the idea meets those needs in a meaningful way.

Market demand is another factor to consider when evaluating ideas. This involves looking at the size and potential of the market, as well as the competition and potential barriers to entry.

Competitive advantage is another factor to consider when evaluating ideas. It's important to consider how the idea compares to what's already available in the market, and whether it offers something unique or different that sets it apart from competitors.

By considering these factors, businesses can identify the ideas with the most potential and focus their efforts on developing and implementing those ideas.

Criteria for evaluating ideas

Factors to consider when evaluating the potential of different ideas, such as feasibility, market demand and cost.

Whether you're a business owner, leader, or individual looking to boost your innovation skills, "Evaluating Ideas" is the ultimate resource for assessing the potential of your ideas.

Evaluating ideas is an important step in the innovation process, as it helps you determine which ideas are worth pursuing and which ones are not. There are a number of criteria that you can use to evaluate the potential of different ideas, including:

- Feasibility: Is it possible to implement the idea, given current resources and constraints?

- Market demand: Is there a market for the idea, and will it meet the needs and preferences of your target audience?

- Cost: What are the costs associated with implementing the idea, and is the potential return on investment sufficient to justify those costs?

- Alignment with company goals: Does the idea align with the overall goals and values of your company, and will it contribute to the company's long-term success?

By considering these and other criteria, you can effectively evaluate the potential of different ideas and select the best ones for further development.

"Evaluating Ideas: A Practical Guide to Assessing the Potential of Your Ideas"

As the CEO of a growing startup, Tia was always on the lookout for new and innovative ideas that could drive success and growth. But with so many ideas to choose from, she found it difficult to determine which ones were worth pursuing. That's when Tia discovered the power of evaluating ideas.

Through the techniques outlined in "Evaluating Ideas," Tia learned how to effectively evaluate the potential of different ideas based on key criteria such as feasibility, market demand, cost, and alignment with company goals. She learned how to use these criteria as a tool to help her select the best ideas for further development.

With the help of this practical guide, Tia was able to transform the way she approached idea selection, leading to a more focused and effective approach to innovation.

Tools for evaluating ideas

Techniques and tools that can be used to evaluate ideas, such as SWOT analysis, and PEST analysis.

Whether you're a business owner, leader, or individual looking to boost your innovation skills, "Evaluating Ideas" is the ultimate resource for assessing the potential of your ideas using tools and techniques.

Evaluating ideas is an important step in the innovation process, as it helps you determine which ideas are worth pursuing and which ones are not. There are a number of tools and techniques that you can use to evaluate ideas, including:

- SWOT analysis: This tool helps you identify the strengths, weaknesses, opportunities, and threats associated with a particular idea. By considering each of these elements, you can get a better understanding of the potential of the idea and how it might fit into your overall business strategy.

- PEST analysis: This tool helps you consider the political, economic, social, and technological factors that could impact the success of an idea. By considering these factors, you can get a better understanding of the potential risks and opportunities associated with the idea.

- Customer journey mapping: This tool helps you understand the different stages that a customer goes through when interacting with your business, and how the idea in question might fit into that journey. This can help you identify opportunities to improve the customer experience and increase customer satisfaction.

- By using tools and techniques such as these, you can more effectively evaluate the potential of different ideas and select the best ones for further development. Other tools and techniques that can be useful for evaluating ideas include:

- Cost-benefit analysis: This tool helps you weigh the costs and benefits of an idea in order to determine its potential value. By considering both the short-term and long-term costs and benefits, you can get a better understanding of the potential return on investment for the idea.

- Business model canvas: This tool helps you identify the key elements of a business model and how they might be affected by an idea. By considering factors such as revenue streams, customer segments, and value proposition, you can get a better understanding of the potential impact of the idea on your business.

- Lean canvas: This tool is similar to the business model canvas but focuses specifically on helping you identify the key risks and uncertainties associated with an idea. By considering these risks and uncertainties, you can more effectively evaluate the feasibility and potential impact of the idea.

By using a variety of tools and techniques, you can effectively evaluate the potential of different ideas and select the best ones for further development.

"Evaluating Ideas: A Practical Guide to Assessing the Potential of Your Ideas Using Tools and Techniques"

As the CEO of a growing startup, Nichosa was always on the lookout for new and innovative ideas that could drive success and growth. But with so many ideas to choose from, she found it difficult to determine which ones were worth pursuing. That's when Nichosa discovered the power of evaluating ideas using tools and techniques.

Through the techniques outlined in "Evaluating Ideas," Nichosa learned how to effectively evaluate the potential of different ideas using a variety of tools and techniques, such as SWOT analysis, PEST analysis, and customer journey mapping. She learned how to use these tools to help her assess the feasibility, market demand, cost, and alignment with company goals of different ideas.

With the help of this practical guide, Nichosa was able to transform the way she approached idea selection, leading to a more focused and effective approach to innovation.

Involving stakeholders in the evaluation process

Strategies for gathering input and feedback from key stakeholders, such as customers, and employees.

Whether you're a business owner, leader, or individual looking to boost your innovation skills, "Evaluating Ideas" is the ultimate resource for assessing the potential of your ideas through stakeholder involvement.

Involving stakeholders in the evaluation process is an important step in the innovation process, as it helps you gather valuable input and feedback that can help you assess the potential of different ideas. There are a number of strategies that you can use to involve stakeholders in the evaluation process, including:

- Customer feedback: By gathering feedback from customers, you can get a better understanding of the potential demand for an idea and how it might meet the needs and preferences of your target audience. This can be done through surveys, focus groups, or other forms of customer research.

- Employee feedback: By gathering feedback from employees, you can get a better understanding of the potential impact of an idea on the company's operations and culture. This can be done through one-on-one conversations, focus groups, or other forms of employee research.

- Investor feedback: By gathering feedback from investors, you can get a better understanding of the potential value of an idea from a financial standpoint. This can be done through one-on-one conversations or presentations to investors.

- Partner feedback: By gathering feedback from partners, such as suppliers or distributors, you can get a better understanding of the potential impact of an idea on your relationships with these key stakeholders. This can be done through one-on-one conversations or presentations to partners.

- Online feedback: By gathering feedback through online channels, such as social media or online surveys, you can get a broad range of input and feedback from a wide variety of stakeholders. This can be a quick and effective way to gather input from a large number of stakeholders in a short amount of time.

By gathering input and feedback from key stakeholders, you can get a more well-rounded understanding of the potential of different ideas and make more informed decisions about which ones to pursue. This can help you select the best ideas for further development and increase the chances of success for your innovation efforts.

"Evaluating Ideas: A Practical Guide to Assessing the Potential of Your Ideas through Stakeholder Involvement"

As the CEO of a growing startup, Twinkle was always on the lookout for new and innovative ideas that could drive success and growth. But with so many ideas to choose from, she found it difficult to determine which ones were worth pursuing.

That's when Twinkle discovered the power of involving stakeholders in the evaluation process.

Through the techniques outlined in "Evaluating Ideas," Twinkle learned how to effectively gather input and feedback from key stakeholders, such as customers, employees, and investors, when evaluating ideas. She learned how to use this input to help her assess the feasibility, market demand, cost, and alignment with company goals of different ideas.

With the help of this practical guide, Twinkle was able to transform the way she approached idea selection, leading to a more focused and effective approach to innovation.

Evaluating the risk profile of different ideas

How to assess the level of risk associated with different ideas and make informed decisions?

Whether you're a business owner, leader, or individual looking to boost your innovation skills, "Evaluating Risk" is the ultimate resource for assessing the risk profile of your ideas.

Evaluating the risk profile of different ideas is an important step in the innovation process, as it helps you assess the potential risks and rewards associated with different ideas and make informed decisions about which ones to pursue. There are a number of tools and techniques that you can use to evaluate the risk profile of different ideas, including:

- Probability analysis: This tool helps you assess the likelihood of different risks occurring, allowing you to prioritize the most significant risks and develop strategies to mitigate them.

- Scenario planning: This technique involves creating hypothetical scenarios based on different risk scenarios and evaluating the potential impacts and responses to those scenarios. This can help you identify potential risks and develop contingency plans to address them.

- Risk matrix: This tool helps you visualize and evaluate the potential risks associated with different ideas by plotting them on a matrix based on their likelihood and impact. This can help you prioritize and address the most significant risks.

- Risk assessment checklist: This tool involves creating a list of potential risks associated with an idea and evaluating them based on their likelihood and impact. This can help you identify and prioritize the most significant risks.

By using tools and techniques like these, you can effectively evaluate the risk profile of different ideas and make informed decisions about which ones to pursue. It's important to keep in mind that all ideas carry some level of risk, and the key is to identify and manage those risks in a way that maximizes the potential rewards.

"Evaluating Risk: A Practical Guide to Assessing the Risk Profile of Your Ideas"

As the CEO of a growing startup, Clinton was always on the lookout for new and innovative ideas that could drive success and growth. But with so many ideas to choose from, he found it difficult to determine which ones were worth pursuing.

That's when Clinton discovered the importance of evaluating the risk profile of different ideas.

Through the techniques outlined in "Evaluating Risk," Clinton learned how to effectively assess the level of risk associated with different ideas and make informed decisions about which ones to pursue. he learned how to use risk assessment tools and techniques, such as probability analysis and scenario planning, to help her evaluate the potential risks and rewards of different ideas.

With the help of this practical guide, Clinton was able to transform the way he approached idea selection, leading to a more focused and effective approach to innovation.

Prioritizing ideas

Techniques for prioritizing ideas based on their potential impact and the resources required to implement them.

Whether you're a business owner, leader, or individual looking to boost your innovation skills, "Prioritizing Ideas" is the ultimate resource for identifying and selecting the best ideas for your business.

Prioritizing ideas is an important step in the innovation process, as it helps you identify and select the best ideas based on their potential impact and the resources required to implement them. There are a number of techniques that you can use to prioritize ideas, including:

- Impact mapping: This technique involves creating a visual representation of the potential impact of different ideas on your business, allowing you to prioritize ideas based on their potential impact.

- Resource allocation analysis: This technique involves analysing the resources required to implement different ideas and prioritizing ideas based on the resources they require. This can help you prioritize ideas that are likely to have the biggest impact with the least number of resources.

- Priority matrix: This tool involves plotting ideas on a matrix based on their potential impact and the resources required to implement them, allowing you to prioritize ideas based on both factors.

- Value proposition analysis: This technique involves evaluating the value that different ideas would bring to your customers, allowing you to prioritize ideas based on their potential to increase customer satisfaction and loyalty.

- 80/20 analysis: This technique involves evaluating the potential impact of different ideas and prioritizing the ones that are likely to have the biggest impact. This can be based on a variety of factors, such as potential return on investment, customer impact, or ease of implementation.

By using techniques like these, you can effectively prioritize ideas and make informed decisions about which ones to pursue. It's important to keep in mind that no single technique is right for every situation, and the key is to use a combination of techniques to get a well-rounded understanding of the potential of different ideas.

"Prioritizing Ideas: A Practical Guide to Identifying and Selecting the Best Ideas for Your Business"

As the CEO of a growing startup, Leo was always on the lookout for new and innovative ideas that could drive success and growth. But with so many ideas to choose from, he found it difficult to determine which ones were worth pursuing. That's when Leo discovered the importance of prioritizing ideas.

Through the techniques outlined in "Prioritizing Ideas," Leo learned how to effectively identify and select the best ideas for his business based on their potential impact and the resources required to implement them. he learned how to use techniques such as impact mapping and resource allocation analysis to help him prioritize ideas and make informed decisions about which ones to pursue.

With the help of this practical guide, Leo was able to transform the way he approached idea selection, leading to a more focused and effective approach to innovation.

Making a business case for selected ideas

How to create a compelling case for investing in a particular idea, including an analysis of the potential?

Whether you're a business owner, leader, or individual looking to boost your innovation skills, "Making the Case" is the ultimate resource for creating a compelling business case for your ideas.

Making a business case for selected ideas is an important step in the innovation process, as it helps you create a compelling argument for investing in a particular idea. There are a number of tools and techniques that you can use to make a business case for your ideas, including:

- Cost-benefit analysis: This tool helps you weigh the costs and benefits of an idea in order to determine its potential value. By considering both the short-term and long-term costs and benefits, you can get a better understanding of the potential return on investment for the idea.

- Return on investment (ROI) calculations: This technique involves calculating the potential financial return on investment for an idea, allowing you to assess the potential value of the idea in terms of its impact on your bottom line.

- SWOT analysis: This tool helps you identify the strengths, weaknesses, opportunities, and threats associated with an idea, allowing you to assess the potential risks and rewards of the idea.

- Customer journey mapping: This technique involves

creating a visual representation of the customer experience with an idea, allowing you to assess the potential value of the idea in terms of customer satisfaction and loyalty.

- Business model canvas: This tool helps you identify the key elements of a business model and how they might be affected by an idea. By considering factors such as revenue streams, customer segments, and value proposition, you can get a better understanding of the potential impact of the idea on your business.

By using tools and techniques like these, you can effectively create a compelling business case for your ideas and make a strong argument for investing in them. It's important to keep in mind that no single tool or technique is right for every situation, and the key is to use a combination of tools and techniques to get a well-rounded understanding of the potential of your ideas.

"Making the Case: A Practical Guide to Creating a Compelling Business Case for Your Ideas"

As the CEO of a growing startup, Andy was always on the lookout for new and innovative ideas that could drive success and growth. But with so many ideas to choose from, she found it difficult to determine which ones were worth pursuing. That's when Andy discovered the importance of making a business case for selected ideas.

Through the techniques outlined in "Making the Case," Andy learned how to effectively create a compelling case for investing in a particular idea, including an analysis of the potential costs and benefits. She learned how to use tools such as cost-benefit analysis and ROI calculations to help her make a strong case for her ideas.

With the help of this practical guide, Andy was able to transform the way she approached idea selection, leading to a more focused and effective approach to innovation.

Managing the portfolio of ideas

Strategies for managing a large pool of ideas and ensuring that the best ones are being pursued.

Whether you're a business owner, leader, or individual looking to boost your innovation skills, "Idea Portfolio Management" is the ultimate resource for managing and maximizing the potential of your ideas.

Managing a large pool of ideas is an important aspect of the innovation process, as it helps you ensure that the best ideas are being pursued and that your resources are being used effectively. There are several strategies that you can use to manage your idea portfolio, including:

- Prioritization matrices: These tools help you prioritize ideas based on their potential impact and the resources required to implement them, allowing you to focus on the most promising ideas.

- Pipeline management: This technique involves creating a structured process for evaluating and selecting ideas for further development, allowing you to manage the flow of ideas through the innovation process.

- Idea banks: These are central repositories for storing and organizing ideas, allowing you to track and manage a large number of ideas effectively.

- Regular review and evaluation: By regularly reviewing and evaluating your idea portfolio, you can identify opportunities for improvement and ensure that you are pursuing the best ideas. This can involve regularly updating your prioritization matrices and pipeline management process to reflect the current state of your ideas.

- Collaboration and idea-sharing: By encouraging collaboration and idea-sharing within your organization, you can tap into the collective knowledge and creativity of your employees and increase the pool of ideas available for consideration.

By using strategies like these, you can effectively manage your idea portfolio and ensure that you are pursuing the best ideas. It's important to keep in mind that managing a large pool of ideas is an ongoing process and requires regular review and evaluation to ensure that you are on track and making progress.

"Idea Portfolio Management: A Practical Guide to Managing and Maximizing the Potential of Your Ideas"

As the CEO of a growing startup, Scot was always on the lookout for new and innovative ideas that could drive success and growth. But with so many ideas to choose from, he found it difficult to determine which ones were worth pursuing and how to manage a large pool of ideas effectively. That's when Scot discovered the importance of idea portfolio management.

Through the techniques outlined in "Idea Portfolio Management," Scot learned how to effectively manage a large pool of ideas and ensure that the best ones were being pursued. he learned how to use tools such as prioritization matrices and pipeline management to help him identify and prioritize the best ideas, and how to create a structured process for evaluating and selecting ideas for further development.

With the help of this practical guide, Scot was able to transform the way he approached idea management, leading to a more focused and effective approach to innovation.

Experimenting with new ideas

Techniques for testing new ideas on a small scale before committing significant resources to them.

Whether you're a business owner, leader, or individual looking to boost your innovation skills, "Idea Experimentation" is the ultimate resource for testing and validating your ideas on a small scale.

Experimenting with new ideas is an important step in the innovation process, as it helps you test and validate your ideas on a small scale before committing significant resources to them. There are several techniques that you can use to experiment with new ideas, including:

- Rapid prototyping: This technique involves creating a quick and simple version of an idea to test and validate it. This can be done using physical prototypes, digital prototypes, or even simple sketches, and allows you to get a sense of how the idea might work in practice.

- A/B testing: This technique involves creating two versions of an idea and testing them against each other to determine which one performs better. This can be done in a variety of contexts, such as website design, marketing campaigns, or product development.

- User testing: This technique involves testing an idea with a small group of users to gather feedback and insights. This can be done through methods such as focus groups, usability testing, or customer interviews, and allows you to gather valuable data about the potential of your idea.

- Pilot programs: This technique involves testing an idea with a small group of customers or users in a real-world setting, allowing you to gather data about how the idea performs in a live environment.

By using techniques like these, you can effectively experiment with new ideas and gather valuable data about their potential. It's important to keep in mind that idea experimentation is an ongoing process and should be incorporated into your regular innovation activities. This allows you to continuously test and validate new ideas, leading to a more focused and effective approach to innovation.

"Idea Experimentation: A Practical Guide to Testing and Validating Your Ideas on a Small Scale"

As the CEO of a growing startup, Helen was always on the lookout for new and innovative ideas that could drive success and growth. But with so many ideas to choose from, she found it difficult to determine which ones were worth pursuing and how to test them effectively. That's when Helen discovered the importance of idea experimentation.

Through the techniques outlined in "Idea Experimentation," Helen learned how to effectively test and validate her ideas on a small scale before committing significant resources to them. She learned how to use tools such as rapid prototyping and A/B testing to quickly and efficiently test her ideas, and how to analyze the results to determine whether an idea was worth pursuing further.

With the help of this practical guide, Helen was able to transform the way she approached idea testing, leading to a more focused and effective approach to innovation.

FOUR

Prototyping and Testing

Strategies for quickly creating prototypes of new ideas and testing them with customers or users to gather feedback.

Prototyping and testing are crucial steps in the innovation process, as they allow businesses to quickly create prototypes of new ideas and gather feedback from customers or users. Prototyping involves creating a physical or digital model of an idea, while testing involves gathering feedback on the prototype from customers or users.

One strategy that businesses can use for prototyping and testing new ideas is starting with low-fidelity prototypes. Low-fidelity prototypes are simple and rough models of an idea and can be created quickly and inexpensively. They are useful for testing the basic concept of an idea and gathering initial feedback. This allows businesses to gather early feedback on their ideas and adjust before investing more time and resources in their development.

Another strategy that businesses can use is agile development methods. Agile development is a flexible and iterative approach to product development that involves creating prototypes, gathering feedback, and iterating on the design. This allows businesses to quickly test and improve their ideas. By using agile development methods, businesses can iterate on their prototypes in real-time and gather continuous feedback from customers or users.

Gathering feedback from customers or users is another important strategy for prototyping and testing new ideas. Customer development techniques involve gathering feedback from customers or users at various stages of the product development process. This can help businesses to identify potential problems and make improvements to the prototype. By gathering feedback from customers or users, businesses can ensure that they are developing products or services that meet the needs and preferences of their target market.

Usability testing is another strategy that businesses can use for prototyping and testing new ideas. Usability testing involves gathering feedback on the usability and user experience of a prototype. This can help businesses to identify any problems with the design and make improvements. By conducting usability testing, businesses can ensure that their prototypes are easy to use and provide a positive user experience.

A/B testing is another strategy that businesses can use for prototyping and testing new ideas. A/B testing involves comparing two versions of a prototype and gathering feedback on which version performs better. This can help businesses to identify the best design for their product or service. By using A/B testing, businesses can gather quantitative data on the performance of different prototypes and make informed decisions about which design to pursue.

Overall, prototyping and testing are crucial steps in the innovation process, as they allow businesses to quickly create prototypes of new ideas and gather feedback from customers or users. By using strategies like low-fidelity prototyping, agile development methods, gathering feedback from customers or users, usability testing, and A/B testing, businesses can ensure that they are developing products or services that meet the needs and preferences of their target market and provide a positive user experience.

Selecting the right prototype for your idea

How to choose the most appropriate type of prototype for your product or idea, based on your goals?

Prototyping is an essential step in the product development process as it allows you to test and validate your product concept. There are several types of prototypes, each with its own set of benefits and drawbacks. Choosing the right prototype for your product or idea can be challenging, but it is crucial for the success of your product. Here are some factors to consider when selecting the most appropriate type of prototype for your product or idea:

- Purpose: The first thing to consider is the purpose of your prototype. Are you looking to test the functionality of your product? Or are you looking to test the design and aesthetics? Different prototypes serve different purposes, and it is essential to choose one that aligns with your goals.

- Resources: Prototyping can be a time-consuming and costly process, so it is important to consider your resources when selecting a prototype. Do you have the necessary skills and equipment to create the prototype yourself, or will you need to outsource the work? Also, consider the time and budget you have available for prototyping.

- Complexity: The complexity of your product will also influence the type of prototype you choose. If your product is relatively simple, a low-fidelity prototype may be sufficient. However, if your product is more complex, you may need a higher-fidelity prototype to fully test and validate your concept.

- Material: The material you use to create your prototype can also impact the effectiveness of the prototype. If you are testing the functionality of your product, you may want to use materials that are similar to those that will be used in the final product. If you are testing the design and aesthetics, you may want to use materials that are easy to work with and modify.

- Testing: Consider how you will be testing your prototype and what type of feedback you are looking to gather. Do you need to test the prototype with users? If so, you may want to create a functional prototype that closely resembles the final product. If you are mainly looking to gather feedback on the design, a visual prototype may be sufficient.

Here are some common types of prototypes and their best uses:

- Sketch prototype: A sketch prototype is a quick and inexpensive way to test and validate your product concept. It is typically created using pencil and paper and is best for testing the overall design and functionality of your product.

- Wireframe prototype: A wireframe prototype is a simple, low-fidelity prototype that is used to test the layout and navigation of a website or mobile app. It is created using wireframing tools and is best for gathering feedback on the user experience.

- 3D printed prototype: A 3D printed prototype is a physical model of your product created using a 3D printer. It is a more realistic representation of your product and is best for testing the form and fit of your product.

- Functional prototype: A functional prototype is a fully functional version of your product that is used to test the functionality and performance of your product. It is typically created using materials similar to those that will be used in the final product and is best for gathering user feedback.

In conclusion, choosing the right prototype for your product or idea is crucial for the success of your product. Consider the purpose, resources, complexity, material, and testing when selecting the most appropriate prototype for your product.

"The right prototype"

As a product designer, Rosey knew the importance of prototyping in the product development process. She had a great idea for a new kitchen gadget, and she was eager to get started on the prototype. However, she wasn't sure which type of prototype would be the most appropriate for her product.

Rosey knew that she wanted to test the functionality of her gadget, as well as gather feedback on the design and aesthetics. She also had a limited budget and time frame for the prototyping process. After some research and consultation with her team, Rosey decided to start with a sketch prototype.

Using pencil and paper, Rosey quickly created a rough sketch of her gadget, including all of the key features and design elements. She then presented the sketch to her team for feedback and discussion. Based on the feedback, Rosey made some adjustments to the design and created a second sketch prototype.

Satisfied with the second sketch prototype, Rosey decided to take it a step further and create a 3D printed prototype. Using a 3D printer, she was able to create a physical model of her gadget, complete with all of the features and design elements. This allowed her to test the form and fit of the product and make any necessary adjustments.

Finally, Rosey and her team were ready to create a functional prototype. Using materials similar to those that would be used in the final product, they built a fully functional version of the gadget. They tested the prototype with several potential customers, gathering valuable feedback on the functionality and performance of the product.

Thanks to careful prototyping, Rosey was able to fine-tune her product and bring it to market successfully. The different types of prototypes allowed her to test and validate her concept at various stages of development, ensuring that the final product met all of her goals and expectations.

Creating prototypes quickly and cheaply

Strategies for creating prototypes on a tight budget and timeline, including tips for repurposing materials.

As you know that prototyping is an essential step in the product development process. It allows you to test and validate your product concept, gather feedback, and make necessary adjustments. However, prototyping can also be a time-consuming and costly process, especially if you are working on a tight budget and timeline.

Here are some strategies for creating prototypes quickly and cheaply:

- Repurpose materials: Instead of buying new materials for your prototype, consider repurposing materials you already have on hand. For example, you can use cardboard, foam board, or recycled materials to create a low-fidelity prototype.

- Use prototyping tools: There are many prototyping tools available that can help you create prototypes quickly and cheaply. For example, wireframing tools allow you to create a low-fidelity prototype of a website or mobile app. 3D printing can also be a cost-effective way to create physical prototypes, especially if you have access to a 3D printer.

- Collaborate with others: Working with a team or collaborating with others can help you share the workload and cost of prototyping. You can also tap into the expertise and resources of others to help you create your prototype.

- Keep it simple: The more complex your prototype, the more time and money it will take to create. Consider starting with a low-fidelity prototype and adding complexity as needed.

- Use virtual prototyping: Virtual prototyping allows you to create a digital version of your product using computer-aided design (CAD) software. This can be a quick and cost-effective way to test and validate your product concept, especially if you are testing the functionality or performance of your product.

"Rapid Prototyping: How to Create Prototypes on a Tight Budget and Timeline"

As the owner of a small design firm, Sandeep was always looking for ways to save time and money on his projects. When he was approached by a client to design a new kitchen gadget, Sandeep knew that prototyping would be an essential part of the process. However, with a tight budget and timeline, he needed to find a way to create prototypes quickly and cheaply.

Sandeep started by repurposing materials he already had on hand, such as cardboard and foam board, to create a low-fidelity prototype of the gadget. he then used a wireframing tool to create a digital prototype of the gadget's user interface.

Next, Sandeep collaborated with a colleague who had access to a 3D printer. Together, they created a 3D printed prototype of the gadget, which allowed them to test the form and fit of the product.

Finally, Sandeep used virtual prototyping to create a digital version of the gadget using CAD software. This allowed him to test the functionality and performance of the product without having to create a physical prototype.

Thanks to Sandeep's clever use of prototyping strategies, he was able to create multiple prototypes on a tight budget and timeline. This helped him to quickly and cost-effectively test and validate his product concept, leading to a successful product launch.

Testing prototypes with users

Techniques for gathering feedback from users, such as user testing, focus groups, and online surveys.

It is crucial to test your prototypes with users to gather valuable feedback and make necessary adjustments. User testing allows you to see how your product is used in the real world and identify any issues or problems that need to be addressed. Here are some techniques for gathering feedback from users:

- User testing: User testing involves observing users as they interact with your prototype and gathering their feedback. This can be done in a controlled setting, such as a lab, or a more natural setting, such as the user's home or office.

- Focus groups: Focus groups are a form of user testing where a group of users is brought together to discuss and provide feedback on your prototype. This can be an effective way to gather a wide range of perspectives and ideas.

- Online surveys: Online surveys are a convenient and cost-effective way to gather feedback from users. You can use tools such as Google Forms or SurveyMonkey to create and distribute surveys to gather feedback on your prototype.

- One-on-one interviews: One-on-one interviews allow you to have a more in-depth conversation with individual users about your prototype. This can be a great way to gather detailed and specific feedback.

"User Testing: Gathering Feedback from Users to

Improve Your Prototype"

As a product designer at a tech startup, Alex was always looking for ways to improve his prototypes. When he was working on a new app, he knew that user testing would be an essential part of the process.

First, Alex conducted user testing in a controlled setting, observing users as they interacted with the app and gathering their feedback. He then held a focus group with a group of users to discuss the app and gather their perspectives.

To reach a wider audience, Alex also created an online survey using Google Forms. He distributed the survey to a large group of users, gathering valuable feedback on the app.

Finally, Alex conducted one-on-one interviews with individual users to gather more detailed and specific feedback.

Thanks to these user testing techniques, Alex was able to gather a wealth of feedback on his app. He used this feedback to make necessary adjustments and improve his prototype, leading to a successful product launch.

Analyzing and interpreting feedback

How to analyze and interpret the feedback you receive from users and use it to make improvements to your prototype?

Gathering feedback from users is an essential part of the prototyping process, but it is only the first step. It is also crucial to analyze and interpret the feedback you receive to make necessary improvements to your prototype. Here are some steps to follow when analyzing and interpreting user feedback:

- Record and organize feedback: Make sure to record all of the feedback you receive, whether it is written or verbal. Organize the feedback into categories or themes to make it easier to analyze.

- Identify patterns: Look for patterns in the feedback you receive. Are there certain issues or problems that are consistently mentioned by users? These are likely areas that need to be addressed.

- Prioritize feedback: Not all feedback will be equally important. Prioritize the feedback based on the impact it will have on your product and the ease of implementation.

- Validate feedback: Don't assume that all feedback is accurate or relevant. Validate the feedback by testing it with additional users or seeking expert opinions.

- Use feedback to make improvements: Use the feedback you receive to make necessary improvements to your prototype. This may involve making changes to the design, functionality, or performance of your product.

"Interpreting Feedback: Using User Feedback to Improve Your Prototype"

As the lead designer at a consumer products company, Prity was always looking for ways to improve her prototypes. When she was working on a new kitchen gadget, she conducted user testing to gather feedback from users.

After the user testing was complete, Prity recorded and organized the feedback she received. She then identified patterns in the feedback, such as common issues or problems with the gadget.

Next, Prity prioritized the feedback based on the impact it would have on the gadget and the ease of implementation. She also validated the feedback by testing it with additional users and seeking expert opinions.

Finally, Prity used the feedback to make necessary improvements to the prototype. She made changes to the design, functionality, and performance of the gadget, resulting in a successful product launch.

Thanks to her careful analysis and interpretation of user feedback, Prity was able to improve her prototype and bring a successful product to market.

Iterating on prototypes

How to incorporate feedback and make changes to your prototypes based on user testing results?

Iterative prototyping is the process of incorporating feedback and making changes to your prototypes based on user testing results. This allows you to continuously improve your product and ensure that it meets the needs and expectations of your users. Here are some steps to follow when iterating on your prototypes:

- Gather feedback: The first step in the iterative prototyping process is to gather feedback from users. This can be done through techniques such as user testing, focus groups, and online surveys.

- Analyze and interpret feedback: Once you have gathered feedback, it is important to analyse and interpret it to identify areas for improvement. Look for patterns in the feedback, prioritize the feedback based on its impact and ease of implementation, and validate the feedback by testing it with additional users or seeking expert opinions.

- Make changes to the prototype: Based on the feedback you receive, make necessary changes to your prototype. This may involve revising the design, functionality, or performance of your product.

- Test the revised prototype: After making changes to your prototype, it is important to test it again with users to gather additional feedback. This will allow you to see if the changes you made were effective and if there are any further areas for improvement.

- Repeat the process: The iterative prototyping process is

ongoing. As you continue to gather and incorporate feedback, you will continually improve your product until it meets the needs and expectations of your users.

"Iterative Prototyping: Incorporating Feedback to Improve Your Product"

As the founder of a small start-up, Tom was always looking for ways to improve his product. When he was working on a new kitchen gadget, he knew that iterative prototyping would be an essential part of the process.

Tom started by conducting user testing to gather feedback on his prototype. He then analysed and interpreted the feedback, identifying areas for improvement. Based on the feedback he received, Tom made changes to the prototype, revising the design, functionality, and performance of the gadget.

Next, Tom tested the revised prototype with users to gather additional feedback. He found that the changes he made had significantly improved the gadget, but there were still a few areas for improvement.

Tom continued the iterative prototyping process, gathering and incorporating additional feedback until he was satisfied with the product. Thanks to iterative prototyping, Tom was able to bring a successful product to market that met the needs and expectations of his users.

Validating prototypes with customers

Strategies for testing prototypes with customers to gather feedback and validate your product or service.

Validating your prototypes with customers is an essential step in the product development process. It allows you to gather feedback from real users and validate your product or service in the market. Here are some strategies for testing prototypes with customers:

- Alpha testing: Alpha testing involves testing your prototype with a small group of customers or users. This can be a good way to gather initial feedback and identify any major issues with your product.

- Beta testing: Beta testing involves testing your prototype with a larger group of customers or users. This allows you to gather more extensive feedback and validate your product in the market.

- Customer discovery: Customer discovery involves conducting interviews or focus groups with customers to gather feedback and validate your product or service. This can be a good way to get a deep understanding of your customers' needs and pain points.

- Customer validation: Customer validation involves testing your prototype with a large group of customers to gather feedback and validate your product in the market. This can help you identify any issues or problems with your product and make necessary adjustments before launch.

"Customer Validation: Testing Your Prototype with

Customers to Gather Feedback and Validate Your Product"

As the CEO of a tech start-up, Nandini was always looking for ways to validate her prototypes with customers. When she was working on a new app, she knew that customer validation would be an essential part of the process.

Nandini started by conducting alpha testing with a small group of users to gather initial feedback on the app. She then conducted beta testing with a larger group of users to gather more extensive feedback.

Next, Nandini conducted customer discovery interviews with a group of customers to gather feedback and validate her product in the market. She found that the feedback she received was extremely valuable and helped her to identify areas for improvement.

Finally, Nandini conducted customer validation with a large group of customers to validate her app in the market. Based on the feedback she received, she made the necessary adjustments to the app and launched it successfully.

Thanks to customer validation, Nandini was able to gather valuable feedback and validate her product in the market, leading to a successful launch. She was able to identify any issues or problems with the app and make necessary adjustments before it went live, ensuring that it met the needs and expectations of her customers. Overall, customer validation was a crucial step in the development process, and Nandini knew that it would be an important aspect of her future product development efforts as well.

Protecting your prototypes

Tips for protecting your prototypes and intellectual property during the testing process.

Prototyping is an essential part of the product development process, but it is also a time when your prototypes and intellectual property are vulnerable. It is important to take steps to protect your prototypes and IP during the testing process to ensure that they are not compromised. Here are some tips for protecting your prototypes and intellectual property:

- Use non-disclosure agreements: A non-disclosure agreement (NDA) is a legal document that prohibits others from disclosing your prototypes or IP. Consider using NDAs when sharing your prototypes or IP with contractors, partners, or other third parties.

- Protect your prototypes physically: Physical prototypes can be easily damaged or stolen. Take steps to protect your prototypes, such as keeping them in a secure location or using security measures like alarms or cameras.

- Use secure communication channels: When sharing your prototypes or IP electronically, make sure to use secure communication channels such as encrypted email or file sharing platforms. This will help protect your prototypes and IP from cyber threats.

- Obtain patents and trademarks: Obtaining patents and trademarks can provide legal protection for your prototypes and IP. This can help prevent others from infringing on your intellectual property and give you legal recourse if your IP is compromised.

- Limit access to prototypes: Only share your prototypes with people who are directly involved in the development process or testing process. The fewer people who have access to your prototypes, the less likely it is that they will be compromised.

- Use dummy prototypes: Consider using dummy prototypes or prototypes with certain features disabled when testing with users. This will allow you to gather valuable feedback without exposing your full prototype or IP.

- Use virtual prototypes: Virtual prototypes, such as those created using computer-aided design (CAD) software, can be a good way to test and validate your product concept without exposing your physical prototypes or IP.

- Protect your online assets: If you have an online presence, make sure to protect your website and social media accounts from cyber threats. Use strong passwords, enable two-factor authentication, and keep your software and security measures up to date.

By following these protection strategies, you can help ensure that your prototypes and intellectual property are safe during the testing process. This will give you the peace of mind to focus on refining and improving your prototypes without worrying about potential threats.

"Protection in Action: Safeguarding Your Prototypes and Intellectual Property during the Testing Process"

As the founder of a small tech start-up, Sam knew that protecting his prototypes and intellectual property was essential. When he was working on a new product, he took several steps to ensure that his prototypes and IP were safe during the testing process

First, Sam used nondisclosure agreements (NDAs) when sharing his prototypes and IP with contractors, partners, and other third parties. He also protected his physical prototypes by keeping them in a secure location and using security measures like alarms and cameras.

When sharing his prototypes and IP electronically, Sam used secure communication channels such as encrypted email and file sharing platforms. He also obtained patents and trademarks to provide legal protection for his prototypes and IP.

In addition to these measures, Sam limited access to his prototypes to only those who were directly involved in the development process. He also used dummy prototypes and virtual prototypes to test and validate his product concept without exposing his full prototypes or IP.

Finally, Sam protected his online assets by using strong passwords, enabling two-factor authentication, and keeping his software and security measures up to date.

Thanks to these protection strategies, Sam was able to safely test and validate his product without worrying about potential threats to his prototypes and IP. As a result, he was able to bring a successful product to market that was protected and secure.

Deciding when to move from prototype to product

How to determine when a prototype is ready to be developed into a full-fledged product or service?

As a product designer or entrepreneur, it is important to know when to move from prototype to product. A prototype is a preliminary model of a product or service that is used to test and validate its concept. When a prototype is ready to be developed into a full-fledged product, it is time to make the transition. Here are some factors to consider when determining when your prototype is ready to become a product:

- Feedback from users: User feedback is crucial in determining the readiness of a prototype. If you have received positive feedback from a significant number of users, it may be time to consider moving your prototype to product.

- Market demand: Is there a demand for your product in the market? If there is a need for your product and you have received positive feedback from users, it may be time to move to product development.

- Technical feasibility: Is your prototype technically feasible? Have you addressed any technical issues or problems that were identified during testing? If your prototype is technically feasible and you have addressed any issues, it may be time to move to product development.

- Resource availability: Do you have the resources necessary to move from prototype to product? This includes financial resources, personnel, and equipment. If you have the necessary resources, it may be time to make the transition.

- Business model: Have you developed a viable business model for your product? If you have a clear plan for how you will generate revenue and sustain your business, it may be time to move to product development.

- Prototype readiness: Is your prototype ready for product development? Have you tested and refined it to the point where it is ready for mass production? If your prototype is ready, it may be time to consider the transition to product.

- Product-market fit: Does your product fit the needs and wants of your target market? If you have conducted market research and determined that there is a good fit, it may be time to consider the transition to product.

- Competitive landscape: How does your product compare to competitors in the market? If your product offers unique features or benefits that set it apart from competitors, it may be time to consider the transition to product.

- Timing: Is the timing right for your product to enter the market? Consider factors such as market trends, seasonal demand, and the timing of other product launches. If the timing is right, it may be time to consider the transition to product.

By considering these additional factors, you can make a well-informed decision about when to move from prototype to product. This will allow you to bring a successful and viable product to market that meets the needs and expectations of your users and has a strong competitive advantage.

"From Prototype to Product: Making the Transition Successfully"

As the CEO of a small tech start-up, Aastha knew that the transition from prototype to product was a crucial step in the product development process. When she was working on a new app, she carefully considered a number of factors to determine when it was time to make the transition.

First, Aastha gathered feedback from users and found that the app received overwhelmingly positive reviews. She also conducted market research and found that there was a high demand for her app in the market.

Next, Aastha evaluated the technical feasibility of her app and addressed any issues or problems that were identified during testing. She also determined that she had the necessary resources, including financial resources, personnel, and equipment, to move from prototype to product.

Aastha also developed a viable business model for her app and conducted a competitive analysis to ensure that it stood out in the market. She also considered the timing of the launch, considering market trends and seasonal demand.

After carefully considering all of these factors, Aastha determined that it was time to make the transition from prototype to product. She successfully launched her app and it quickly gained popularity in the market.

Thanks to her careful planning and consideration of key factors, Aastha was able to make a successful transition from prototype to product. As a result, she was able to bring a successful and viable app to market that met the needs and expectations of her users.

FIVE

Implementing New Ideas

Tips for successfully launching and scaling new products or processes within an organization.

Implementing new ideas is an important step in the innovation process, as it involves launching and scaling new products or processes within an organization. Successfully implementing new ideas requires careful planning and execution, as well as a willingness to adapt and pivot as needed.

One tip for successfully implementing new ideas is to clearly define the goals and objectives of the new idea. It's important to have a clear understanding of the goals and objectives of the new idea, as this will help to guide the implementation process and ensure that resources are allocated appropriately. Having a clear set of goals and objectives can also help to ensure that the new idea aligns with the overall strategy and goals of the organization.

Another tip is to develop a detailed implementation plan. A detailed implementation plan should outline the steps required to launch and scale the new idea, as well as the resources needed to do so. This can help to ensure that the implementation process runs smoothly and efficiently and can help to identify potential challenges or roadblocks that may arise.

Communicating with stakeholders is another important tip for successfully implementing new ideas. It's important to keep stakeholders informed about the progress of the new idea and any potential impacts it may have. This can help to build support and ensure that everyone is on the same page. It's also important to be open to feedback and ideas from stakeholders, as they may have valuable insights that can help to improve the new idea.

Being prepared to pivot is another tip that can help businesses to successfully implement new ideas. It's important to be willing to pivot and adjust the implementation plan as needed. Things may not always go according to plan and being open to change, and adaptability can help to ensure the success of the new idea. This may involve making changes to the scope of the project, adjusting the timeline, or changing the resources allocated to the project.

Finally, it's important to monitor and evaluate the success of the new idea. This involves regularly reviewing the progress of the new idea and adjusting as needed. It's important to track key metrics and indicators of success and to use this data to inform future decisions about the new idea. By regularly monitoring and evaluating the success of the new idea, businesses can ensure that it is meeting its goals and objectives and that resources are being used effectively.

Developing a rollout plan

How to create a detailed plan for launching and scaling a new product or process, including timelines and budget?

Developing a rollout plan is an essential step in the product development process. It helps you to create a detailed plan for launching and scaling a new product or process, including timelines, budgets, and resources. Here are eight key elements to consider when developing a rollout plan:

- Objectives: What are the goals of your rollout plan? Be specific and clearly define your objectives. This will help you to measure the success of your rollout.

- Timelines: When do you plan to launch your product or process? Create a timeline that outlines the key milestones and deadlines for your rollout.

- Budget: How much do you plan to spend on your rollout? Create a budget that outlines the resources, such as personnel, equipment, and marketing, that you will need to launch and scale your product or process.

- Resources: What resources will you need to successfully rollout your product or process? This includes personnel, equipment, and materials. Make sure to allocate sufficient resources to ensure the success of your rollout.

- Marketing: How will you promote your product or process to customers? Develop a marketing plan that outlines the strategies and tactics you will use to reach your target audience.

- Training: Will you need to train your personnel or customers on your product or process? Create a training plan that outlines the training materials and resources that will be needed.

- Rollout team: Who will be responsible for executing the rollout plan? Identify the key team members and allocate responsibilities to ensure that all aspects of the rollout are covered.

- Contingency plan: What will you do if something goes wrong during the rollout? Develop a contingency plan that outlines the steps you will take to mitigate any potential issues or problems.

By considering these key elements, you can create a detailed rollout plan that will help ensure the success of your product or process launch. This will allow you to bring your product or process to market in an organized and efficient manner.

"Rollout Success: Creating a Detailed Plan for Launching and Scaling a New Product"

As the CEO of a small tech start-up, Selva knew that developing a rollout plan was crucial to the success of his new product. When he was preparing to launch a new app, he spent a significant amount of time creating a detailed rollout plan.

First, Selva defined the objectives of his rollout plan. He wanted to launch the app and achieve a certain number of downloads within the first six months. He also wanted to generate a certain amount of revenue from the app within the first year.

Next, Selva created a timeline that outlined the key milestones and deadlines for his rollout. He also developed a budget that outlined the resources, such as personnel, equipment, and marketing, that he would need to launch and scale his app.

Selva also identified the resources that he would need to successfully rollout his app, including personnel, equipment, and materials. He developed a marketing plan to promote the app to customers and created a training plan to ensure that his personnel were prepared to support the app.

Selva also identified the key team members who would be responsible for executing the rollout plan and allocated responsibilities to ensure that all aspects of the rollout were covered. Finally, he developed a contingency plan in case anything went wrong during the rollout.

Thanks to his detailed rollout plan, Selva was able to successfully launch his app and achieve his objectives. The app quickly gained popularity in the market and generated a significant amount of revenue for Selva's company.

Communicating the change

Strategies for communicating the change and the benefits of the new product or process to stakeholders, such as employees.

Communicating the change and the benefits of a new product or process to stakeholders is an essential aspect of the rollout process. Stakeholders, such as employees, customers, and investors, need to be informed and prepared for the change for it to be successful. Here are eight strategies for communicating the change and the benefits of a new product or process to stakeholders:

- Communicate the benefits: Clearly explain the benefits of the new product or process to stakeholders. This includes how it will improve efficiency, increase productivity, or provide value to customers.

- Involve stakeholders in the process: Involve stakeholders in the rollout process to ensure that they are informed and invested in the change. This can be done through regular communication, workshops, or focus groups.

- Communicate the timeline: Communicate the timeline for the rollout to stakeholders. This will help them to understand the timing of the change and any deadlines that need to be met.

- Address concerns: Address any concerns that stakeholders may have about the change. This can include addressing any potential disruptions or challenges that may arise.

- Use multiple channels: Use multiple channels to communicate the change to stakeholders. This can include emails, newsletters, social media, and in-person meetings.

- Provide training and support: Provide training and support to stakeholders to ensure that they are prepared for the change. This can include providing resources such as training materials or offering training sessions to help stakeholders understand the new product or process.

- Highlight success stories: Share success stories or case studies to demonstrate the benefits of the new product or process. This can help to build support and enthusiasm for the change.

- Communicate regularly: Regular communication is key to ensuring that stakeholders are informed and prepared for the change. Make sure to keep stakeholders updated on the progress of the rollout and any updates or changes that may arise.

By following these strategies, you can effectively communicate the change and the benefits of a new product or process to stakeholders. This will help to ensure that the rollout is successful and that stakeholders are on board with the change.

"Communicating Change: A Success Story"

As the CEO of a small tech company, Maria knew that communicating the change and the benefits of a new product to stakeholders was crucial to its success. When she was preparing to launch a new app, she developed a comprehensive plan to communicate the change to employees, customers, and investors.

First, Maria communicated the benefits of the new app to stakeholders. She explained how the app would improve efficiency, increase productivity, and provide value to customers. She also involved stakeholders in the rollout process through regular communication, workshops, and focus groups.

Maria also communicated the timeline for the rollout to stakeholders, addressing any concerns they may have had about the change. She used multiple channels, including emails, newsletters, and social media, to keep stakeholders informed and updated on the progress of the rollout.

To ensure that stakeholders were prepared for the change, Maria provided training and support through resources such as training materials and training sessions. She also shared success stories and case studies to demonstrate the benefits of the new app.

Through her comprehensive and well-planned communication strategy, Maria was able to effectively communicate the change and the benefits of the new app to stakeholders. As a result, the rollout was successful, and the app quickly gained popularity in the market.

Training and onboarding

How to provide training and support to ensure that employees are prepared to implement the new product or process effectively?

Providing training and support to employees is essential to ensure that they are prepared to implement a new product or process effectively. By offering training and onboarding resources, you can help employees to understand the new product or process and how to use it effectively. Here are ten key considerations for providing training and onboarding to your employees:

- Identify training needs: Identify the specific training needs of your employees. This can include understanding the new product or process, learning how to use it effectively, and understanding any associated policies or procedures.

- Develop a training plan: Develop a training plan that outlines the training materials, resources, and activities that will be provided to employees. This should include both in-person and online training options.

- Consider different learning styles: Consider the different learning styles of your employees when developing your training plan. This can include visual, auditory, and kinaesthetic learners.

- Use a variety of training methods: Use a variety of training methods, such as lectures, hands-on exercises, and simulations, to engage employees and ensure that they are retaining the information.

- Provide ongoing support: Provide ongoing support to employees after the initial training period. This can include access to resources such as training materials or support from a mentor or supervisor.

- Assess effectiveness: Assess the effectiveness of your training program to ensure that employees are retaining the information and are able to apply it in their work.

- Onboard new employees: Make sure to provide onboarding resources and support to new employees to help them understand the company culture, policies, and procedures. This can include training sessions, mentorship programs, and access to resources such as employee handbooks.

- Foster a culture of learning: Foster a culture of learning within your organization to encourage continuous learning and development. This can include providing access to training resources, encouraging employees to take on new challenges, and recognizing their efforts.

- Invest in leadership development: Invest in leadership development programs to ensure that your leaders are equipped to lead and support their teams through the implementation of a new product or process.

- Communicate expectations: Clearly communicate the expectations and goals for the new product or process to employees. This will help them to understand their role in the implementation process and how they can contribute to its success.

By considering these key factors, you can provide effective training and onboarding to ensure that your employees are prepared to implement a new product or process effectively. This will help to ensure the success of the rollout and the adoption of the new product or process within your organization.

"Training and Onboarding: Ensuring Successful Implementation of a New App"

As the CEO of a small tech company, Shreya knew that providing training and onboarding to her employees was essential to ensure the successful implementation of a new app. When she was preparing to launch the app, she developed a comprehensive training and onboarding plan to ensure that her employees were prepared to use it effectively.

First, Shreya identified the specific training needs of her employees, including understanding the features and functionality of the app, as well as any associated policies and procedures. She then developed a training plan that included both in-person and online training options and considered the different learning styles of her employees.

Shreya used a variety of training methods, including lectures, hands-on exercises, and simulations, to engage her employees and ensure that they were retaining the information. She also provided ongoing support, including access to training materials and support from a mentor or supervisor.

To ensure the success of the new app, Shreya also provided onboarding resources and support to new employees and fostered a culture of learning within the organization. She invested in leadership development programs and clearly communicated the expectations and goals for the new app to her employees.

Thanks to her comprehensive training and onboarding plan, Shreya's employees were able to effectively implement the new app and it quickly gained popularity in the market. The app's success was a testament to Shreya's commitment to ensuring that her employees were prepared and supported throughout the rollout process.

The Destined Innovator

Managing resistance to change

Tips for addressing and overcoming resistance to change within an organization.

Managing resistance to change is an important aspect of the rollout process. It is common for employees to resist change, especially if they are not fully prepared or if they are unsure of the benefits of the new product or process. Here are tips for addressing and overcoming resistance to change within an organization:

- Communicate clearly: Clearly communicate the reasons for the change and the benefits it will bring to employees. This will help to build understanding and support for the change.

- Involve employees in the process: Involve employees in the rollout process to ensure that they are informed and invested in the change. This can be done through regular communication, workshops, or focus groups.

- Address concerns: Address any concerns that employees may have about the change. This can include addressing any potential disruptions or challenges that may arise.

- Provide training and support: Provide training and support to employees to ensure that they are prepared for the change. This can include providing resources such as training materials or offering training sessions to help employees understand the new product or process.

- Offer ongoing support: Offer ongoing support to employees after the initial rollout period. This can include access to resources such as training materials or support from a mentor or supervisor.

- Highlight success stories: Share success stories or case studies to demonstrate the benefits of the new product or process. This can help to build support and enthusiasm for the change.

- Communicate regularly: Regular communication is key to ensuring that employees are informed and prepared for the change. Make sure to keep employees updated on the progress of the rollout and any updates or changes that may arise.

- Emphasize the importance of change: Emphasize the importance of change and the benefits it will bring to the organization. This can help to build a culture of innovation and continuous improvement.

- Encourage a growth mindset: Encourage a growth mindset within the organization to foster a positive attitude towards change. This can involve providing opportunities for learning and development and recognizing employees for their efforts.

- Provide leadership and support: Provide leadership and support to employees throughout the change process. This can include offering guidance, answering questions, and addressing any concerns they may have.

By following these tips, you can effectively manage resistance to change and overcome any obstacles to the successful rollout of a new product or process. This will help to ensure the success of the rollout and the adoption of the new product or process within your organization.

Addressing and overcoming resistance

As the CEO of a small tech company, Sarah knew that managing resistance to change was an important aspect of the rollout process. When she was preparing to launch a new app, she developed a comprehensive plan to address and overcome resistance to change within the organization.

First, Sarah clearly communicated the reasons for the change and the benefits of the new app to her employees. She involved them in the rollout process through regular communication, workshops, and focus groups, and addressed any concerns they may have had about the change.

Sarah provided training and support to her employees to ensure that they were prepared for the change, including access to training materials and support from a mentor or supervisor. She also offered ongoing support and shared success stories to demonstrate the benefits of the new app.

To encourage a positive attitude towards change, Sarah emphasized the importance of the new app and the benefits it would bring to the organization. She fostered a culture of innovation and continuous improvement by encouraging a growth mindset within the company and recognizing employees for their efforts.

Thanks to her comprehensive approach to managing resistance to change, Sarah was able to successfully rollout the new app and achieve her objectives. The app quickly gained popularity in the market and generated a significant amount of revenue for the company. Sarah's success was a testament to her ability to effectively manage resistance to change and overcome any obstacles to the rollout process.

Monitoring and measuring

success:

Techniques for tracking the performance of the new product or process and identifying areas for improvement.

Monitoring and measuring the performance of a new product or process is essential to ensure its success and identify areas for improvement. By tracking key metrics and collecting feedback from stakeholders, you can gain valuable insights into the performance of the new product or process and make any necessary adjustments. Here are techniques for monitoring and measuring success:

- Identify key performance indicators (KPIs): Identify the key performance indicators (KPIs) that will be used to track the performance of the new product or process. These should be aligned with the objectives of the rollout and should be measurable and actionable.

- Set benchmarks: Set benchmarks for the performance of the new product or process to provide a baseline for comparison. These benchmarks should be based on industry standards or previous performance data.

- Collect data: Collect data on the performance of the new product or process using the KPIs and benchmarks that have been identified. This can be done through automated tracking systems or manual data collection methods.

- Analyze data: Analyze the data collected to identify trends and patterns in the performance of the new product or process. This can be done through visualizing the data using charts and graphs or through statistical analysis.

- Identify areas for improvement: Identify areas for improvement based on the data analysis. This can include identifying areas where performance is not meeting expectations or identifying opportunities for optimization.

- Set improvement goals: Set improvement goals based on the areas for improvement that have been identified. These goals should be specific, measurable, achievable, relevant, and time-bound (SMART).

- Implement improvement actions: Implement improvement actions to address the areas for improvement and achieve the improvement goals that have been set. This can include making changes to the new product or process, implementing new policies or procedures, or providing additional training and support.

- Track progress: Track progress towards the improvement goals on an ongoing basis to ensure that the actions being taken are having the desired impact. This can be done through regular data collection and analysis.

- Gather feedback: Gather feedback from stakeholders, including employees, customers, and investors, to understand their experiences with the new product or process and identify any additional areas for improvement.

- Communicate results: Communicate the results of the monitoring and measurement efforts to stakeholders to keep them informed of the performance of the new product or process and any improvements that have been made.

By following these techniques, you can effectively monitor and measure the performance of a new product or process and identify areas for improvement. This will help to ensure the success of the rollout and the long-term success of the new product or process within your organization.

"Monitoring and Measuring Success: Achieving Ongoing Improvement in Product Performance"

As the CEO of a small tech company, Tushar knew that monitoring and measuring the performance of his new product was essential to its success. When he was preparing to launch a new app, he developed a comprehensive plan to track its performance and identify areas for improvement.

First, Tushar identified the key performance indicators (KPIs) that would be used to track the performance of the new app. He set benchmarks based on industry standards and previous performance data and collected data on the app's performance using automated tracking systems.

Using the data that he collected, Tushar analysed the performance of the app to identify trends and patterns. He identified areas for improvement, including areas where performance was not meeting expectations, and set specific, measurable, achievable, relevant, and time-bound (SMART) improvement goals.

To achieve these improvement goals, Tushar implemented a variety of improvement actions, including making changes to the app, implementing new policies and procedures, and providing additional training and support to his employees. He tracked progress towards the improvement goals on an ongoing basis and gathered feedback from stakeholders to understand their experiences with the app and identify any additional areas for improvement.

Thanks to Tushar's comprehensive approach to monitoring and measuring success, the performance of the new app continuously improved over time. The app became a popular choice in the market and generated a significant amount of revenue for the company. Tushar's success was a testament to his ability to effectively track the performance of his product and identify opportunities for improvement.

Managing the transition

Strategies for managing the transition from the old product or process to the new one, including strategies for phasing out.

Managing the transition from an old product or process to a new one is an important aspect of the rollout process. It is important to have a plan in place to ensure a smooth and seamless transition, and to minimize disruption and downtime. Here are strategies for managing the transition:

- Develop a phased approach: Develop a phased approach to the transition to minimize disruption and ensure that the new product or process is fully tested and refined before it is fully implemented.

- Communicate the transition plan: Communicate the transition plan to all stakeholders, including employees, customers, and investors. This will help to ensure that everyone is informed and prepared for the change.

- Provide training and support: Provide training and support to employees to ensure that they are prepared for the transition. This can include providing resources such as training materials or offering training sessions to help employees understand the new product or process.

- Address any concerns: Address any concerns that employees or customers may have about the transition. This can include addressing any potential disruptions or challenges that may arise.

- Test the new product or process: Test the new product or process to ensure that it is fully functional and ready for implementation. This can include conducting user testing or pilot programs to gather feedback and make any necessary adjustments.

- Plan for downtime: Plan for any potential downtime during the transition period to ensure that it is minimized and managed effectively. This can include having a backup plan in place or providing support to customers during any disruptions.

- Monitor progress: Monitor progress towards the transition goals on an ongoing basis to ensure that the transition is on track and any issues are addressed in a timely manner.

- Gather feedback: Gather feedback from stakeholders during the transition period to understand their experiences with the new product or process and identify any areas for improvement

- Phase out the old product or process: Phase out the old product or process in a controlled and orderly manner to ensure that it is fully replaced by the new one. This can include providing support to customers during the transition period and developing a plan for decommissioning the old product or process.

- Celebrate successes: Celebrate successes and milestones during the transition period to keep stakeholders motivated and engaged. This can include recognizing the efforts of employees or hosting events to mark the transition to the new product or process.

By following these strategies, you can effectively manage the transition from an old product or process to a new one and minimize disruption and downtime. This will help to ensure the success of the rollout and the long-term success of the new product or process within your organization.

"Managing the Transition: Smoothly Phasing Out the Old and Phasing in the New"

As the CEO of a small tech company, Julie knew that managing the transition from an old product to a new one was an important aspect of the rollout process. When she was preparing to launch a new app, she developed a comprehensive plan to ensure a smooth and seamless transition.

First, Julie developed a phased approach to the transition, which allowed her to test and refine the new app before it was fully implemented. She communicated the transition plan to all stakeholders and provided training and support to her employees to ensure that they were prepared for the change.

To minimize disruption and downtime, Julie addressed any concerns that employees or customers may have had about the transition and tested the new app to ensure that it was fully functional. She also planned for any potential downtime and monitored progress towards the transition goals on an ongoing basis.

As part of the transition, Julie phased out the old product in a controlled and orderly manner and provided support to customers during the transition period. She celebrated successes and milestones along the way, which helped to keep stakeholders motivated and engaged.

Thanks to Julie's comprehensive approach to managing the transition, the rollout of the new app was a success. The app quickly gained popularity in the market and generated a significant amount of revenue for the company. Julie's success was a testament to her ability to smoothly phase out the old and phase in the new and minimize disruption and downtime.

Managing risk

How to identify and mitigate potential risks associated with implementing a new product or process?

Managing risk is an important aspect of the rollout process, as it helps to ensure the success of a new product or process and minimize any negative impacts. By identifying and mitigating potential risks, you can reduce the likelihood of unexpected problems or challenges arising. Here are strategies for managing risk:

- Identify potential risks: Identify potential risks associated with implementing a new product or process by considering factors such as the impact on customers, employees, and stakeholders, and the potential impact on the organization.

- Assess the likelihood and impact of each risk: Assess the likelihood and impact of each identified risk to prioritize which risks should be addressed first.

- Develop risk mitigation strategies: Develop strategies to mitigate the identified risks, such as implementing controls or procedures, or establishing contingency plans.

- Communicate the risk management plan: Communicate the risk management plan to all stakeholders to ensure that everyone is aware of the potential risks and the strategies that have been put in place to mitigate them.

- Monitor and review the risk management plan: Monitor and review the risk management plan on an ongoing basis to ensure that it remains effective, and any new risks are identified and addressed.

- Establish a system for reporting risks: Establish a system for employees to report any potential risks that they identify and ensure that all reports are promptly addressed.

- Provide training on risk management: Provide training to employees on risk management to ensure that they are aware of the potential risks associated with their work and how to identify and address them.

- Conduct risk assessments regularly: Conduct risk assessments regularly to identify any new or emerging risks that may not have been previously identified.

- Review and update policies and procedures: Review and update policies and procedures to ensure that they are aligned with the risk management plan and address any identified risks.

- Establish contingency plans: Establish contingency plans to ensure that the organization is prepared to respond effectively to any unexpected events or challenges that may arise.

By following these strategies, you can effectively manage risk and ensure the success of a new product or process. This will help to minimize any negative impacts and maximize the potential for success.

"Managing Risk: A Success Story in Product Rollout"

As the CEO of a small tech company, Varun knew that managing risk was an important aspect of the rollout process. When he was preparing to launch a new app, he developed a comprehensive plan to identify and mitigate potential risks.

First, Varun identified potential risks associated with the rollout of the new app, including the impact on customers and employees, and the potential impact on the organization. He assessed the likelihood and impact of each risk and developed strategies to mitigate them, such as implementing controls and procedures, and establishing contingency plans.

Varun communicated the risk management plan to all stakeholders and established a system for employees to report any potential risks that they identified. He provided training on risk management to his employees and conducted risk assessments regularly to ensure that all potential risks were identified and addressed.

Thanks to Varun's comprehensive approach to managing risk, the rollout of the new app was a success. The app quickly gained popularity in the market and generated a significant amount of revenue for the company. Varun's success was a testament to his ability to effectively identify and mitigate potential risks and ensure the success of the rollout.

Continuous improvement

Strategies for continually improving the new product or process over time.

Continuous improvement is an important aspect of the rollout process, as it helps to ensure that a new product or process remains relevant and effective over time. By continually improving the new product or process, you can increase customer satisfaction, enhance employee productivity, and increase the overall success of the product or process. Here are strategies for continuous improvement:

- Identify areas for improvement: Identify areas for improvement by gathering feedback from customers, employees, and stakeholders, and analysing data on the performance of the new product or process.

- Set improvement goals: Set specific, measurable, achievable, relevant, and time-bound (SMART) improvement goals based on the areas for improvement that have been identified.

- Implement improvement actions: Implement improvement actions to address the identified areas for improvement and achieve the improvement goals that have been set. This can include making changes to the new product or process, implementing new policies or procedures, or providing additional training and support.

- Monitor progress: Monitor progress towards the improvement goals on an ongoing basis to ensure that the actions being taken are having the desired impact. This can be done through regular data collection and analysis.

- Gather feedback: Gather feedback from stakeholders, including employees, customers, and investors, to understand their experiences with the new product or process and identify any additional areas for improvement.

- Incorporate new technologies: Incorporate new technologies and best practices into the new product or process to enhance its performance and stay ahead of the competition.

- Encourage innovation: Encourage innovation and continuous learning within the organization to promote a culture of continuous improvement.

- Establish metrics for success: Establish metrics for success to track the performance of the new product or process and identify areas for improvement.

- Conduct regular reviews: Conduct regular reviews of the new product or process to identify any changes or improvements that may be necessary.

- Foster a culture of continuous improvement: Foster a culture of continuous improvement within the organization by promoting a focus on ongoing improvement and recognizing the efforts of employees who contribute to improvement efforts.

By following these strategies, you can ensure that the new product or process is continually improved over time. This will help to increase customer satisfaction, enhance employee productivity, and increase the overall success of the product or process.

"Continuous Improvement: Achieving Ongoing

Success through Constant Evolution"

As the CEO of a small tech company, Sierra knew that continuous improvement was an important aspect of the rollout process. When she was preparing to launch a new app, she developed a comprehensive plan to continually improve the app over time.

First, Sierra identified areas for improvement by gathering feedback from customers and analysing data on the performance of the app. She set specific, measurable, achievable, relevant, and time-bound (SMART) improvement goals based on the identified areas and implemented improvement actions to achieve these goals.

To monitor progress, Sierra regularly collected data on the performance of the app and gathered feedback from stakeholders. She also incorporated new technologies and best practices into the app to enhance its performance and stay ahead of the competition.

Sierra fostered a culture of continuous improvement within the organization by encouraging innovation and continuous learning and establishing metrics for success. She conducted regular reviews of the app to identify any changes or improvements that may be necessary and recognized the efforts of employees who contributed to improvement efforts.

Thanks to Sierra's comprehensive approach to continuous improvement, the performance of the new app continuously improved over time. The app became a popular choice in the market and generated a significant amount of revenue for the company. Sierra's success was a testament to her ability to continually improve the app and achieve ongoing success

SIX

Overcoming Barriers to Innovations

Strategies for dealing with common obstacles to innovation such as risk aversion, lack of resources.

Innovation is essential for businesses to stay competitive and relevant, but it can be difficult to bring new ideas to fruition. There are a variety of barriers that businesses may face when trying to innovate, including risk aversion, lack of resources, and resistance to change.

One strategy for overcoming barriers to innovation is to create a culture that supports risk-taking and experimentation. This involves encouraging employees to come up with new ideas and providing the support and resources they need to test and develop those ideas. It also involves creating an environment where it's okay to fail, as failure can often be a valuable learning opportunity.

Another strategy is to allocate resources specifically for innovation. This can include setting aside a budget for prototyping and testing new ideas, as well as dedicating time and personnel to work on innovation projects. By providing the resources needed to bring new ideas to fruition, businesses can increase their chances of success.

Another strategy is to address resistance to change. It's natural for people to resist change, but it's important to address this resistance and find ways to overcome it. This may involve educating employees about the benefits of the new idea, seeking support from key stakeholders, or making changes to the implementation process to address concerns or issues.

Overall, there are a variety of strategies that businesses can use to overcome barriers to innovation. By creating a culture that supports risk-taking and experimentation, allocating resources specifically for innovation, and addressing resistance to change, businesses can increase their chances of success and drive innovation within their organization.

Risk aversion

Strategies for overcoming a culture of risk aversion and encouraging employees to take calculated risks and propose new ideas.

Overcoming a culture of risk aversion is an important aspect of the rollout process, as it helps to ensure that new ideas and opportunities are explored and pursued. By encouraging employees to take calculated risks and propose new ideas, you can foster innovation and increase the chances of success for the new product or process. Here are strategies for overcoming risk aversion:

- Communicate the importance of risk-taking: Communicate the importance of risk-taking and innovation to the success of the organization to encourage a culture of risk-taking.

- Establish a supportive culture: Establish a supportive culture that encourages employees to take calculated risks and propose new ideas and provides resources and support to help them do so.

- Encourage transparency: Encourage transparency and open communication within the organization to create an environment where employees feel comfortable sharing ideas and voicing concerns.

- Provide training: Provide training on risk assessment and management to help employees understand how to identify and evaluate potential risks, and how to mitigate them.

- Encourage diversity: Encourage diversity within the organization to foster a range of perspectives and ideas and create a culture of inclusivity and innovation.

- Establish clear goals and objectives: Establish clear goals and objectives for the new product or process to provide a clear direction and focus for innovation efforts.

- Recognize and reward risk-takers: Recognize and reward employees who take calculated risks and propose new ideas to encourage a culture of risk-taking.

- Foster collaboration: Foster collaboration within the organization to encourage the sharing of ideas and the development of new solutions.

- Establish a process for evaluating and implementing new ideas: Establish a process for evaluating and implementing new ideas to ensure that they are thoroughly considered and given the opportunity to succeed.

- Create a safe space for experimentation: Create a safe space for experimentation where employees can test and refine new ideas without fear of failure.

By following these strategies, you can overcome a culture of risk aversion and encourage employees to take calculated risks and propose new ideas. This will foster innovation and increase the chances of success for the new product or process.

"Overcoming Risk Aversion: A Story of Innovation and Success"

As the CEO of a small tech company, Jason knew that overcoming a culture of risk aversion was an important aspect of the rollout process. When he was preparing to launch a new app, he developed a comprehensive plan to encourage his employees to take calculated risks and propose new ideas.

First, Jason communicated the importance of risk-taking and innovation to the success of the organization and established a supportive culture that encouraged employees to take calculated risks and propose new ideas. He encouraged transparency and open communication within the organization and provided training on risk assessment and management to help employees understand how to identify and evaluate potential risks.

Jason also encouraged diversity within the organization and established clear goals and objectives for the new app. He recognized and rewarded employees who took calculated risks and proposed new ideas and fostered collaboration within the organization to encourage the sharing of ideas and the development of new solutions.

Jason also established a process for evaluating and implementing new ideas and created a safe space for experimentation where employees could test and refine new ideas without fear of failure.

Thanks to Jason's comprehensive approach to overcoming risk aversion, the rollout of the new app was a success. The app quickly gained popularity in the market and generated a significant amount of revenue for the company. Jason's success was a testament to his ability to foster innovation and encourage his employees to take calculated risks, leading to a culture of success and growth.

Lack of resources

Techniques for maximizing limited resources and finding creative solutions to resource constraints.

Finding creative solutions to resource constraints is an important aspect of the rollout process, as it helps to ensure that new products or processes can be implemented effectively, despite any limitations. By maximizing limited resources and finding creative solutions, you can increase the chances of success for the new product or process. Here are techniques for maximizing limited resources:

- Identify key resources: Identify the key resources that are necessary for the successful rollout of the new product or process and prioritize them.

- Assess resource availability: Assess the availability of the identified key resources and identify any potential shortages or constraints.

- Develop contingency plans: Develop contingency plans to address potential shortages or constraints, such as identifying alternative resources or implementing cost-saving measures.

- Leverage existing resources: Leverage existing resources, such as equipment, technology, and personnel, to the fullest extent possible to maximize efficiency and minimize costs.

- Utilize partnerships: Utilize partnerships with other organizations or individuals to access additional resources or expertise.

- Repurpose materials: Repurpose materials or equipment

whenever possible to reduce the need for new resources.

- Implement cost-saving measures: Implement cost-saving measures, such as reducing waste or streamlining processes, to maximize efficiency and minimize resource utilization.

- Encourage resourcefulness: Encourage resourcefulness and creativity within the organization to find innovative solutions to resource constraints.

- Utilize technology: Utilize technology, such as cloud-based solutions, to access resources and expertise remotely, without the need for additional physical resources.

- Seek external funding: Seek external funding, such as grants or investments, to access additional resources and support.

By following these techniques, you can maximize limited resources and find creative solutions to resource constraints. This will increase the chances of success for the new product or process, despite any limitations.

"Maximizing Limited Resources: A Story of Success Despite Constraints"

As the CEO of a small tech company, Rachel knew that finding creative solutions to resource constraints was an important aspect of the rollout process. When she was preparing to launch a new app, she faced significant resource constraints, including a limited budget and a small team.

To address these constraints, Rachel developed contingency plans to address potential shortages and leveraged her existing resources to the fullest extent possible. She utilized partnerships with other organizations to access additional resources and expertise and repurposed materials and equipment whenever possible to reduce the need for new resources.

Rachel also implemented cost-saving measures, such as reducing waste and streamlining processes, to maximize efficiency and minimize resource utilization. She encouraged resourcefulness and creativity within the organization to find innovative solutions to resource constraints and utilized technology to access resources and expertise remotely.

When these strategies proved insufficient, Rachel sought external funding in the form of grants and investments to access additional resources and support.

Thanks to Rachel's comprehensive approach to maximizing limited resources, the rollout of the new app was a success. Despite the significant resource constraints, Rachel was able to find creative solutions and successfully launch the app in the market. Her success was a testament to her ability to find innovative ways to overcome resource constraints and achieve success.

Resistance to change

Tips for addressing and overcoming resistance to change, including strategies for communication and engagement.

Overcoming resistance to change is an important aspect of the rollout process, as it helps to ensure that new products or processes are successfully implemented and adopted. By addressing and overcoming resistance to change, you can increase the chances of success for the new product or process. Here are tips for overcoming resistance to change:

- Communicate the rationale for change: Clearly communicate the rationale for change to employees, including the benefits of the new product or process and how it will impact the organization.

- Involve employees in the change process: Involve employees in the change process by seeking their input and feedback and providing them with opportunities to contribute to the implementation of the new product or process.

- Provide training and support: Provide training and support to help employees understand and adapt to the new product or process and address any concerns they may have.

- Address concerns and objections: Address concerns and objections that employees may have about the change and address any underlying issues or needs that may be causing resistance.

- Offer incentives: Offer incentives, such as recognition or rewards, to encourage employees to embrace the change.

- Establish clear goals and objectives: Establish clear goals and objectives for the new product or process to provide a clear direction and focus for the change effort.

- Foster a culture of transparency: Foster a culture of transparency and open communication to create an environment where employees feel comfortable voicing their concerns and ideas.

- Emphasize the benefits of change: Emphasize the benefits of change, such as increased efficiency or customer satisfaction, to encourage employees to embrace the new product or process.

- Foster a culture of continuous improvement: Foster a culture of continuous improvement to encourage a focus on ongoing improvement and change.

- Encourage leadership and ownership: Encourage leadership and ownership among employees to encourage a sense of responsibility for the success of the new product or process.

By following these tips, you can overcome resistance to change and increase the chances of success for the new product or process.

"Overcoming Resistance to Change: A Story of Successful Implementation"

As the CEO of a small tech company, Jeniffer knew that overcoming resistance to change was an important aspect of the rollout process. When he was preparing to launch a new app, he faced significant resistance from his employees, who were hesitant to embrace the change.

To address this resistance, Jeniffer clearly communicated the rationale for change to his employees, including the benefits of the new app and how it would impact the organization. He involved them in the change process by seeking their input and feedback, and provided them with training and support to help them understand and adapt to the new app.

Jeniffer also addressed concerns and objections that his employees had about the change, and offered incentives, such as recognition and rewards, to encourage them to embrace it. He established clear goals and objectives for the new app and fostered a culture of transparency and open communication to create an environment where employees felt comfortable voicing their concerns and ideas.

Jeniffer emphasized the benefits of change, such as increased efficiency and customer satisfaction, and fostered a culture of continuous improvement to encourage a focus on ongoing improvement and change. He also encouraged leadership and ownership among his employees, to encourage a sense of responsibility for the success of the new app.

Thanks to Jeniffer's comprehensive approach to overcoming resistance to change, the rollout of the new app was a success. His employees were able to adapt to the new app and embrace the change, leading to increased efficiency and customer satisfaction for the company. Jeniffer's success was a testament to his ability to effectively address and overcome resistance to change and implement new products or processes successfully.

Limited time and attention

Strategies for prioritizing innovation efforts and ensuring that they get the time and attention they need.

Maximizing limited time and attention is an important aspect of the rollout process, as it helps to ensure that new products or processes get the focus and support, they need to be successful. By prioritizing innovation efforts and ensuring that they get the time and attention they need, you can increase the chances of success for the new product or process. Here are strategies for maximizing limited time and attention:

- Identify key priorities: Identify the key priorities for the rollout of the new product or process and prioritize them accordingly.

- Set clear goals and objectives: Set clear goals and objectives for the new product or process to provide a clear direction and focus for innovation efforts.

- Allocate resources appropriately: Allocate resources, such as personnel and budget, appropriately to ensure that the key priorities receive the necessary support and attention.

- Establish clear roles and responsibilities: Establish clear roles and responsibilities to ensure that everyone knows what is expected of them, and to minimize duplication of efforts.

- Foster collaboration and teamwork: Foster collaboration and teamwork to encourage the sharing of ideas and the development of new solutions.

- Encourage delegation: Encourage delegation to allow key personnel to focus on the key priorities, and to help develop the skills and expertise of others.

- Utilize technology: Utilize technology, such as project management tools, to streamline processes and maximize efficiency.

- Implement time management strategies: Implement time management strategies, such as prioritizing tasks and setting deadlines, to ensure that the key priorities receive the necessary attention.

- Set aside dedicated time for innovation: Set aside dedicated time for innovation to encourage a focus on ongoing improvement and change.

- Encourage a culture of continuous improvement: Encourage a culture of continuous improvement to foster a focus on ongoing improvement and change.

By following these strategies, you can maximize limited time and attention and increase the chances of success for the new product or process.

"Maximizing Limited Time and Attention: A Story of Success Despite Constraints"

As the CEO of a small tech company, Jenny knew that maximizing limited time and attention was an important aspect of the rollout process. When she was preparing to launch a new app, she faced significant constraints, including a tight timeline and a limited budget.

To address these constraints, Jenny identified the key priorities for the rollout of the new app and set clear goals and objectives to provide a clear direction and focus for innovation efforts. She allocated resources appropriately to ensure that the key priorities received the necessary support and attention and established clear roles and responsibilities to minimize duplication of efforts.

Jenny fostered collaboration and teamwork within the organization to encourage the sharing of ideas and the development of new solutions and encouraged the delegation to allow key personnel to focus on the key priorities. She utilized technology to streamline processes and maximize efficiency and implemented time management strategies to ensure that the key priorities received the necessary attention.

Jenny also set aside dedicated time for innovation and encouraged a culture of continuous improvement to foster a focus on ongoing improvement and change.

Thanks to Jenny's comprehensive approach to maximizing limited time and attention, the rollout of the new app was a success. Despite the significant constraints, Jenny was able to prioritize her efforts and ensure that the key priorities received the necessary support and attention. Her success was a testament to her ability to effectively manage limited time and attention and achieve success despite constraints.

Limited knowledge and skills:

Tips for building the knowledge and skills needed to generate and implement innovative ideas.

Building knowledge and skills is an important aspect of the rollout process, as it helps to ensure that you have the expertise and capabilities needed to generate and implement innovative ideas. By building the knowledge and skills needed to generate and implement innovative ideas, you can increase the chances of success for the new product or process. Here are tips for building knowledge and skills:

- Identify knowledge and skills gaps: Identify the knowledge and skills gaps within the organization and determine what is needed to fill those gaps.

- Seek out training and development opportunities: Seek out training and development opportunities, such as workshops and courses, to build the knowledge and skills needed to generate and implement innovative ideas.

- Utilize technology: Utilize technology, such as online learning platforms and resources, to access knowledge and skills remotely.

- Encourage lifelong learning: Encourage lifelong learning within the organization and provide employees with the support and resources they need to continue learning and growing.

- Foster a culture of continuous improvement: Foster a culture of continuous improvement to encourage a focus on ongoing learning and development.

- Utilize mentorship and coaching: Utilize mentorship and

coaching to provide employees with guidance and support as they build their knowledge and skills.

- Engage with experts: Engage with experts in the field to access their knowledge and expertise, and to learn from their experiences.

- Collaborate with other organizations: Collaborate with other organizations to access their knowledge and resources, and to learn from their experiences.

- Encourage networking: Encourage networking within the organization, and with external organizations, to access new knowledge and connections.

- Encourage experimentation and risk-taking: Encourage experimentation and risk-taking to foster a culture of innovation and encourage the development of new skills.

By following these tips, you can build the knowledge and skills needed to generate and implement innovative ideas and increase the chances of success for the new product or process.

"Building Knowledge and Skills: A Story of Successful Innovation"

As the CEO of a small tech company, Mira knew that building knowledge and skills was an important aspect of the rollout process. When she was preparing to launch a new app, she recognized that her team had some knowledge and skills gaps that needed to be filled in order to successfully generate and implement innovative ideas.

To address these gaps, Mira sought out training and development opportunities, such as workshops and courses, to build the knowledge and skills needed for the rollout of the new app. She utilized technology, such as online learning platforms and resources, to access knowledge and skills remotely, and encouraged lifelong learning within the organization to ensure that her team was constantly learning and growing.

Mira fostered a culture of continuous improvement and utilized mentorship and coaching to provide her team with guidance and support as they built their knowledge and skills. She engaged with experts in the field and collaborated with other organizations to access their knowledge and resources. She encouraged networking within the organization, and with external organizations, to access new knowledge and connections.

Finally, Mira encouraged experimentation and risk-taking to foster a culture of innovation and encourage the development of new skills.

Thanks to Mira's comprehensive approach to building knowledge and skills, the rollout of the new app was a success. Her team was able to generate and implement innovative ideas, leading to increased efficiency and customer satisfaction for the company. Mira's success was a testament to her ability to effectively build the knowledge and skills needed to achieve success.

Limited access to customers and markets

Strategies for gathering customer feedback and testing ideas in the market, even if access is limited.

Gathering customer feedback and testing ideas in the market is an important aspect of the rollout process, as it helps to validate the new product or process and ensure that it meets the needs of the target market. By gathering customer feedback and testing ideas in the market, you can increase the chances of success for the new product or process. Here are strategies for gathering customer feedback and testing ideas in the market, even if access is limited:

- Utilize online research tools: Utilize online research tools, such as surveys and focus groups, to gather customer feedback and test ideas remotely.

- Leverage social media: Leverage social media to access customers and gather feedback, and to test ideas with a larger audience.

- Utilize customer service channels: Utilize customer service channels, such as phone and email, to gather customer feedback and test ideas.

- Collaborate with partners: Collaborate with partners, such as distributors and retailers, to access their customer base and gather feedback.

- Conduct market research: Conduct market research to gather data and insights about the target market, and to identify opportunities for testing ideas.

- Utilize customer advisory councils: Utilize customer advisory councils to gather feedback and test ideas with a small group of dedicated customers.

- Attend industry events: Attend industry events to access customers and gather feedback, and to test ideas with a larger audience.

- Utilize customer feedback loops: Utilize customer feedback loops, such as feedback forms and surveys, to gather ongoing feedback and test ideas.

- Engage with influencers: Engage with influencers to access their audience and gather feedback, and to test ideas with a larger audience.

- Utilize prototypes: Utilize prototypes to gather feedback and test ideas with customers, even if access is limited.

By following these strategies, you can gather customer feedback and test ideas in the market, even if access is limited, and increase the chances of success for the new product or process.

"Gathering Customer Feedback and Testing Ideas: A Story of Success Despite Constraints"

As the CEO of a small tech company, Sarah knew that gathering customer feedback and testing ideas in the market was an important aspect of the rollout process. When she was preparing to launch a new app, she faced significant constraints, including limited access to customers and markets.

To address these constraints, Sarah utilized online research tools, such as surveys and focus groups, to gather customer feedback and test ideas remotely. She leveraged social media to access customers and gather feedback and utilized customer service channels to gather ongoing feedback.

Sarah also collaborated with partners, such as distributors and retailers, to access their customer base and gather feedback. She conducted market research to gather data and insights about the target market and utilized customer advisory councils to gather feedback and test ideas with a small group of dedicated customers.

Sarah attended industry events to access customers and gather feedback and utilized customer feedback loops to gather ongoing feedback and test ideas. She engaged with influencers to access their audience and gather feedback and utilized prototypes to gather feedback and test ideas with customers, even if access was limited.

Thanks to Sarah's comprehensive approach to gathering customer feedback and testing ideas in the market, the rollout of the new app was a success. Despite the significant constraints, Sarah was able to gather valuable feedback and test ideas with customers, leading to increased efficiency and customer satisfaction for the company. Sarah's success was a testament to her ability to effectively gather customer feedback and test ideas in the market, even when access was limited.

Limited support from leadership

Tips for building support for innovation from leadership and decision-makers.

Building support for innovation from leadership and decision-makers is an important aspect of the rollout process, as it helps to ensure that the new product or process has the necessary resources and backing to succeed. By building support for innovation, you can increase the chances of success for the new product or process. Here are tips for building support for innovation from leadership and decision-makers:

- Communicate the value proposition: Clearly communicate the value proposition of the new product or process to leadership and decision-makers and highlight the benefits it will bring to the organization.

- Utilize data and research: Utilize data and research to support your case for innovation, and to demonstrate the potential for success.

- Engage leadership and decision-makers early: Engage leadership and decision-makers early in the process and involve them in the development and planning stages.

- Align with organizational goals: Align the new product or process with organizational goals and objectives and highlight how it will contribute to the overall success of the organization.

- Utilize champions: Utilize champions within the organization to help build support for innovation, and to advocate for the new product or process.

- Involve leadership and decision-makers in the testing and

validation process: Involve leadership and decision-makers in the testing and validation process and provide them with the opportunity to see the new product or process in action.

- Utilize storytelling: Utilize storytelling to engage leadership and decision-makers, and to highlight the potential impact of the new product or process.

- Communicate progress and successes: Communicate progress and successes throughout the rollout process and highlight the positive impact of the new product or process.

- Manage expectations: Manage expectations and be transparent about any challenges or setbacks that may arise.

- Seek feedback and input: Seek feedback and input from leadership and decision-makers throughout the rollout process and incorporate their insights and recommendations.

By following these tips, you can build support for innovation from leadership and decision-makers and increase the chances of success for the new product or process.

"Building Support for Innovation: A Story of Successful Engagement"

As the CEO of a small tech company, Kellie knew that building support for innovation from leadership and decision-makers was an important aspect of the rollout process. When she was preparing to launch a new app, she recognized that she needed to build support for innovation in order to ensure that the new product had the necessary resources and backing to succeed.

To build support for innovation, Kellie clearly communicated the value proposition of the new app to leadership and decision-makers and highlighted the benefits it would bring to the organization. She utilized data and research to support her case for innovation and engaged leadership and decision-makers early in the process, involving them in the development and planning stages.

Kellie aligned the new app with organizational goals and objectives and utilized champions within the organization to help build support for innovation. She involved leadership and decision-makers in the testing and validation process, and utilized storytelling to engage them and highlight the potential impact of the new app.

Throughout the rollout process, Kellie communicated progress and successes, and managed expectations by being transparent about any challenges or setbacks that arose. She sought feedback and input from leadership and decision-makers and incorporated their insights and recommendations.

Thanks to Kellie's efforts to build support for innovation, the rollout of the new app was a success. Leadership and decision-makers were fully engaged and invested in the new product, and the organization saw increased efficiency and customer satisfaction as a result. Kellie's success was a testament to her ability to effectively build support for innovation from leadership and decision-makers.

Competition

Strategies for staying ahead of the competition and finding new ways to differentiate your products or services.

Staying ahead of the competition is an important aspect of the rollout process, as it helps to ensure that your products or services remain competitive in the market. By staying ahead of the competition, you can increase the chances of success for the new product or process. Here are strategies for staying ahead of the competition and finding new ways to differentiate your products or services:

- Utilize market research: Utilize market research to gather data and insights about the competitive landscape, and to identify opportunities for differentiation.

- Leverage customer feedback: Leverage customer feedback to identify areas for improvement and to differentiate your products or services.

- Utilize data analytics: Utilize data analytics to identify trends and patterns in customer behavior, and to differentiate your products or services.

- Engage with industry influencers: Engage with industry influencers to stay informed about the latest trends and developments, and to differentiate your products or services.

- Collaborate with partners: Collaborate with partners to access new markets and differentiate your products or services.

- Utilize design thinking: Utilize design thinking to identify new solutions and to differentiate your products or services.

- Utilize agile development: Utilize agile development to iterate quickly and to differentiate your products or services.

- Utilize customer segmentation: Utilize customer segmentation to tailor your products or services to specific market segments, and to differentiate your offerings.

- Utilize content marketing: Utilize content marketing to build a strong brand and to differentiate your products or services.

- Utilize personalization: Utilize personalization to tailor your products or services to individual customers, and to differentiate your offerings.

By following these strategies, you can stay ahead of the competition and find new ways to differentiate your products or services, increasing the chances of success for the new product or process.

"Staying Ahead of the Competition: A Story of Successful Differentiation"

As the CEO of a small tech company, Tom knew that staying ahead of the competition was an important aspect of the rollout process. When he was preparing to launch a new app, he faced significant competition in the market.

To stay ahead of the competition, Tom utilized market research to gather data and insights about the competitive landscape and leveraged customer feedback to identify areas for improvement. He utilized data analytics to identify trends and patterns in customer behaviour and engaged with industry influencers to stay informed about the latest trends and developments.

Tom collaborated with partners to access new markets and utilized design thinking to identify new solutions. He utilized agile development to iterate quickly and utilized customer segmentation to tailor his app to specific market segments.

Tom utilized content marketing to build a strong brand and utilized personalization to tailor his app to individual customers. Thanks to Tom's efforts to differentiate his app, the rollout was a success, and the app gained a significant share of the market. Tom's success was a testament to his ability to stay ahead of the competition and find new ways to differentiate his products or services.

SEVEN

The Role of Leadership in Fostering Innovation

Strategies for leaders to support and encourage innovation within their organizations.

Leadership plays a crucial role in fostering innovation within an organization. Leaders have the ability to create an environment that encourages creativity and risk-taking and can help to drive the development of new ideas and processes.

One strategy that leaders can use to support and encourage innovation is to set a clear vision for the organization that inspires and motivates employees. This vision should be aligned with the values and goals of the organization and should provide a clear direction for innovation efforts.

Another strategy is to create a culture that values creativity and innovation. This involves encouraging employees to come up with new ideas and providing the resources and support they need to test and develop those ideas. It also involves creating an environment where it's okay to fail, as failure can often be a valuable learning opportunity.

Leaders can also play a role in driving innovation by acting as champions for new ideas and processes. This involves advocating for new ideas and providing the resources and support needed to bring them to fruition. It also involves recognizing and rewarding employees who come up with new ideas and contribute to the innovation process.

Finally, leaders can foster innovation by encouraging collaboration and cross-functional teamwork. Innovation often requires input and expertise from a variety of disciplines, and leaders can create opportunities for employees from different departments to work together and share ideas.

Overall, the role of leadership in fostering innovation is crucial. By setting a clear vision, creating a culture that values creativity and innovation, acting as champions for new ideas, and encouraging collaboration and cross-functional teamwork, leaders can support and encourage innovation within their organization.

Setting the vision and direction

How leaders can set a clear vision and direction for innovation within their organization?

Setting a clear vision and direction for innovation is an important aspect of leadership, as it helps to ensure that the organization can evolve setting a visual direction for innovation, leaders can inspire and guide the efforts of their teams and increase the chances of success for new products and processes. Here are tips for setting the vision and direction for innovation within an organization:

- Communicate the importance of innovation: Clearly Communication of innovation to the organization, and the role it plays in driving growth and success.
- Set clear goals and objectives: Set clear goals and objectives for innovation and ensure that they align with the overall vision and mission of the organization.
- Establish a culture of innovation: Establish a culture of innovation within the organization and encourage employees to generate and share new ideas.
- Encourage risk-taking: Encourage risk-taking and experimentation and create a safe space for employees to explore and test new ideas.
- Foster collaboration: Foster collaboration and cross-functional teamwork and encourage employees from different departments and teams to work together on innovation projects.
- Encourage continuous learning: Encourage continuous learning and development and provide resources and support for employees to learn new skills and stay up to date on industry trends.
- Utilize design thinking: Utilize design thinking to identify new solutions and to fast innovation within the organization.

- Utilize agile development: Utilize agile development to iterate quickly and to fostering innovation within the organization.
- Foster a customer-centric approach: Foster a customer-centric approach and encourage employees to gather feedback and insights from customers to inform innovation efforts.
- Encourage networking and partnerships: Encourage networking and partnerships, and foster relationships with external organizations and individuals to bring new ideas and perspectives into the organization.
- Utilize technology: Utilize technology to facilitate innovation and provide employees with access to the tools and resources they need to generate and test new ideas.
- Encourage leadership at all levels: Encourage leadership at all levels and empower employees at all levels of the organization to contribute to the innovation process.
- Provide resources and support: Provide resources and support for innovation projects, including funding, time, and other resources as needed.
- Encourage **transparency**: Encourage transparency and create a culture of open communication and sharing of ideas.
- Encourage experimentation: Encourage experimentation and testing of new ideas and create a culture of continuous improvement.
- Recognize and reward innovation: Recognize and reward innovation and celebrate the successes and achievements of employees who contribute to the innovation process.
- Encourage diversity and inclusion: Encourage diversity and inclusion and seek out diverse perspectives and ideas to foster innovation within the organization.
- Foster a growth mindset: Foster a growth mindset and encourage employees to embrace change and

continuously learn and improve.
- Encourage continuous feedback: Encourage continuous feedback and communication and seek out regular feedback from employees to inform the innovation process.
- Lead by example: Lead by example and demonstrate a commitment to innovation through your own actions and behaviors.

By following these tips, leaders can set the vision and direction for innovation within their organization and foster a culture of continuous improvement and innovation.

"Setting the Vision and Direction: A Story of Successful Innovation Leadership"

As the CEO of a small tech company, Genelia knew that fostering innovation was critical to the long-term success of the organization. When she took over as CEO, she made it a priority to set a clear vision and direction for innovation within the company.

Genelia communicated the importance of innovation to the organization and set clear goals and objectives for innovation efforts. She established a culture of innovation within the company and encouraged employees to generate and share new ideas. She encouraged risk-taking and experimentation and created a safe space for employees to explore and test new ideas.

Genelia fostered collaboration and cross-functional teamwork and encouraged employees from different departments and teams to work together on innovation projects. She also encouraged continuous learning and development and provided resources and support for employees to learn new skills and stay up to date on industry trends.

Genelia utilized design thinking and agile development to foster innovation within the company and encouraged a customer-centric approach to inform innovation efforts. She encouraged networking and partnerships and fostered relationships with external organizations and individuals to bring new ideas and perspectives into the company.

Genelia utilized technology to facilitate innovation and provided employees with access to the tools and resources they needed to generate and test new ideas. She encouraged leadership at all levels, and empowered employees at all levels of the organization to contribute to the innovation process.

Thanks to Genelia's efforts to set the vision and direction for innovation within the company, the organization was able to adapt and evolve over to significant growth and success as a result. Genelia's success was a testament to her ability to foster innovation within the organization, and t lead by example in driving continuous improvement and innovation.

Leading by example

Ways that leaders can model and encourage a culture of innovation within their organization.

Leading by example is an important aspect of fostering a culture of innovation within an organization. By modelling and encouraging a culture of innovation, leaders can inspire and guide the efforts of their teams and increase the chances of success for new products and processes. Here are ways that leaders can lead by example and model a culture of innovation within their organization:

- Communicate the importance of innovation: Clearly communicate the importance of innovation to the organization, and the role it plays in driving growth and success.

- Set clear goals and objectives: Set clear goals and objectives for innovation and ensure that they align with the overall vision and mission of the organization.

- Foster collaboration: Foster collaboration and cross-functional teamwork and encourage employees from different departments and teams to work together on innovation projects.

- Encourage continuous learning: Encourage continuous learning and development and provide resources and support for employees to learn new skills and stay up to date on industry trends.

- Utilize design thinking: Utilize design thinking to identify new solutions and to foster innovation within the organization.

- Utilize agile development: Utilize agile development to iterate quickly and to foster innovation within the organization.

- Foster a customer-centric approach: Foster a customer-centric approach and encourage employees to gather feedback and insights from customers to inform innovation efforts.

- Encourage networking and partnerships: Encourage networking and partnerships, and foster relationships with external organizations and individuals to bring new ideas and perspectives into the organization.

- Utilize technology: Utilize technology to facilitate innovation and provide employees with access to the tools and resources they need to generate and test new ideas.

- Encourage continuous feedback: Encourage continuous feedback and communication and seek out regular feedback from employees to inform the innovation process.

- Encouraged risk-taking: Ferry encouraged risk-taking and experimentation and created a safe space for employees to explore and test new ideas.

- Encouraged transparency: Ferry encouraged transparency and created a culture of open communication and sharing of ideas.

- Encouraged experimentation: Ferry encouraged experimentation and testing of new ideas and created a culture of continuous improvement.

- Recognized and rewarded innovation: Ferry recognized and rewarded innovation and celebrated the successes and achievements of employees who contributed to the innovation process.

- Encouraged diversity and inclusion: Ferry encouraged diversity and inclusion and sought out diverse perspectives and ideas to foster innovation within the organization.

- Foster a growth mindset: Ferry fostered a growth mindset and encouraged employees to embrace change and continuously learn and improve.

- Encouraged leadership at all levels: Ferry encouraged leadership at all levels, and empowered employees at all levels of the organization to contribute to the innovation process.

- Provided resources and support: Ferry provided resources and support for innovation projects, including funding, time, and other resources as needed.

- Demonstrated a commitment to innovation: Ferry demonstrated a commitment to innovation through her own actions and behaviours and made it a priority to stay up to date on industry trends and best practices.

- Encouraged continuous feedback: Ferry encouraged continuous feedback and communication and sought out regular feedback from employees to inform the innovation process.

By leading by example and modelling a culture of innovation, leaders can inspire and guide the efforts of their teams and increase the chances of success for new products and processes.

"Leading by Example: A Story of Successful Innovation Culture"

As the CEO of a small tech company, Ferry knew that fostering a culture of innovation was critical to the long-term success of the organization.

Ferry made it a priority to lead by example and model a culture of innovation within the company. She communicated the importance of innovation to the organization and set clear goals and objectives for innovation efforts. She fostered collaboration and cross-functional teamwork and encouraged employees from different departments and teams to work together on innovation projects.

Ferry encouraged continuous learning and development and provided resources and support for employees to learn new skills and stay up to date on industry trends. She utilized design thinking and agile development to foster innovation within the company and encouraged a customer-centric approach to inform innovation efforts.

Ferry encouraged networking and partnerships, and fostered relationships with external organizations and individuals to bring new ideas and perspectives into the company. She utilized technology to facilitate innovation and provided employees with access to the tools and resources they needed to generate and test new ideas.

Thanks to Ferry's efforts to lead by example and model a culture of innovation within the company, the organization was able to adapt and evolve over time and saw significant growth and success as a result. Ferry's success was a testament to her ability to foster a culture of innovation within the organization, and to lead by example in driving continuous improvement and innovation.

Providing resources and support

Strategies for providing the resources and support that employee need to generate and pursue new ideas.

Providing the right resources and support is crucial for fostering a culture of innovation within an organization. By giving employees the tools and resources, they need to generate and pursue new ideas, leaders can increase the chances of success for innovation projects and drive growth and success for the organization. Here are ways that leaders can provide the resources and support that employees need to generate and pursue new ideas:

- Set a clear vision and direction for innovation: Leadership needs to establish a clear vision and direction for innovation within the organization so that everyone is working towards the same goals.

- Encourage creativity: Encourage employees to think creatively and look for new and innovative ways to solve problems.

- Provide resources and support: Provide employees with the resources and support they need to generate and pursue new ideas, such as an innovation fund, access to industry experts and thought leaders, and dedicated time for idea generation and brainstorming.

- Foster a culture of continuous improvement: Encourage employees to test and iterate on their ideas and recognize and reward innovation.

- Empower employees to take ownership of their ideas: Give employees the autonomy to pursue their ideas and take ownership of them.

- Encourage cross-functional collaboration: Encourage employees from different departments to work together and share ideas.

- Encourage outside-the-box thinking: Encourage employees to think outside the box and consider unconventional approaches to problem-solving.

- Encourage employees to challenge the status quo: Encourage employees to question the status quo and look for ways to improve existing processes and products.

- Encourage employees to take on new challenges: Encourage employees to take on new challenges and take on roles outside of their comfort zones to stimulate creative thinking.

- Encourage a diverse and inclusive workplace: Foster a diverse and inclusive workplace, as diverse perspectives and backgrounds can lead to more innovative ideas.

- Encourage learning and development: Provide employees with opportunities for learning and development, such as training and education programs, to help them develop the skills and knowledge needed to generate and pursue new ideas.

- Encourage employee engagement: Engage employees in the innovation process by soliciting their input and ideas and involving them in decision-making.

- Encourage risk-taking: Encourage employees to take calculated risks and reward them for their efforts, even if their ideas don't succeed.

- Encourage a culture of experimentation: Encourage employees to experiment and test new ideas to learn and improve.

- Encourage open communication: Foster an open and transparent communication culture, where employees feel comfortable sharing their ideas and concerns.

- Encourage leadership involvement: Encourage leadership to be involved in the innovation process and provide support and guidance to employees.

- Encourage a culture of continuous learning: Foster a culture of continuous learning, where employees are encouraged to seek out new knowledge and skills to stay ahead of the competition.

- Encourage employees to seek out new opportunities: Encourage employees to seek out new opportunities and look for ways to expand the business into new markets or sectors.

- Encourage customer focus: Encourage employees to focus on customer needs and gather customer feedback to inform innovation efforts.

- Encourage a culture of innovation throughout the organization: Foster a culture of innovation throughout the organization, from leadership down to entry-level employees.

By providing the right resources and support, leaders can create an environment that fosters innovation and encourages employees to generate and pursue new ideas. This can increase the chances of success for innovation projects and drive growth and success for the organization.

"Empowering Innovation: A Story of Providing Resources and Encouragement for Employee Ideas"

As the CEO of a mid-sized manufacturing company, Ray knew that fostering a culture of innovation was essential for the long-term success of the business. He made it a priority to provide his employees with the resources and support they needed to generate and pursue new ideas.

One of the first things Ray did was establish an innovation fund, which provided funding for employee-led innovation projects. He also provided his team with access to industry experts and thought leaders, who could provide guidance and support as they developed their ideas.

In addition to providing financial resources, Ray also made sure to allocate time for his team to focus on innovation. He dedicated a portion of each week to brainstorming sessions and idea-generation workshops, which allowed his employees to think creatively and collaborate.

To encourage risk-taking and experimentation, Ray fostered a culture of continuous improvement and encouraged his team to test and iterate on their ideas. He recognized and rewarded innovation and celebrated the successes of employees who generated and pursued new ideas.

Ray also made sure to empower his employees to take ownership of their ideas and gave them the autonomy to pursue them. He encouraged cross-functional collaboration and encouraged employees from different departments to work together and share ideas.

Thanks to Ray's efforts to provide resources and support for innovation, the company was able to develop several successful new products and processes and saw significant growth as a result. Ray's success was a testament to the importance of providing resources and support for employee ideas and fostering a culture of innovation within an organization.

Encouraging risk-taking and experimentation

How leaders can create an environment that encourages risk-taking and experimentation to employees?

As a leader, it's your job to create an environment that encourages risk-taking and experimentation. But how do you do this? How do you support your employees when their ideas don't succeed?

In this book, we'll explore practical strategies that you can use to create a culture of risk-taking and experimentation within your organization. From setting clear expectations around failure to providing resources and support for experimentation, we'll cover a range of tactics that you can use to encourage your team to think outside the box and try new things.

- Set clear expectations around failure: Make it clear to your employees that it's okay to take risks and experiment, even if those efforts don't succeed.

- Provide resources for experimentation: Give your employees the resources they need to try new things, such as a budget for prototyping and testing, access to software and tools, and training in design thinking and creative problem-solving.

- Encourage a growth mindset: A growth mindset, or the belief that one's abilities can be developed through effort and learning, is correlated with increased creativity and innovation. Encourage your employees to adopt a growth mindset by providing training and development opportunities and promoting a culture of continuous learning.

- Foster a culture of transparency: A culture of transparency can help to create a sense of trust and collaboration within your organization. Encourage open communication and be transparent about the successes and failures of your team.

- Celebrate failure: Don't be afraid to celebrate the failures of your team, as long as they are accompanied by lessons learned. This can help to create a culture where failure is seen as a normal part of the process of innovation.

- Provide support: When an employee's idea doesn't succeed, make sure to provide support and guidance to help them learn from the experience and move forward.

- Encourage risk-taking: To generate new ideas and pursue innovation, it's important to be opened to taking risks.

- Encourage open and honest communication and feedback, which allowed employees to feel safe sharing their ideas and concerns.

- Establish clear goals and objectives, which provided a framework for employees to test and validate their ideas.

- Reward and recognize employees for their contributions, which encouraged them to take risks and experiment with new ideas.

" How the Fail Fast initiative helped Kaif's agency became more comfortable with taking risks and trying new things"

As the CEO of a marketing agency, Kaif was always looking for ways to stay ahead of the curve and come up with innovative campaigns for his clients. He knew that in order to do this, his team needed to be comfortable with taking risks and trying new things.

One day, Kaif decided to implement a new policy at the agency. He called it the "Fail Fast" initiative, and the idea was simple: encourage employees to take risks and experiment with new ideas and support them when those ideas didn't succeed.

To make sure that everyone was on board with this new policy, Kaif held a meeting with the entire team to explain the reasoning behind it. "I know that it can be scary to try new things and take risks," he said. "But the reality is that in order to come up with truly innovative ideas, we need to be comfortable with failure. That's why I'm implementing the Fail Fast initiative. It's okay to fail, as long as we learn from our mistakes and keep moving forward."

Kaif also provided resources to support employees in their experimentation, such as a budget for prototyping and testing, and training in design thinking and creative problem-solving.

As a result of the Fail Fast initiative, the team at the agency became more comfortable with taking risks and trying new things. They came up with a number of successful campaigns that had never been done before, and the agency saw a significant increase in business as a result.

Fostering collaboration and idea sharing

Tips for creating a culture of openness and collaboration where employees feel comfortable sharing ideas.

The modern workplace is constantly evolving and becoming more complex. With the advent of technology and the proliferation of remote work, it has become increasingly important for organizations to foster a culture of openness and collaboration. When employees feel comfortable sharing their ideas and working with others to develop them, it can lead to increased innovation and productivity. In this book, we will explore 20 tips for creating a culture of collaboration and idea sharing in your organization.

- Encourage open communication: Create an environment where employees feel comfortable sharing their ideas, asking questions, and giving feedback.

- Foster teamwork: Encourage employees to work together and support each other in achieving common goals.

- Encourage creativity: Set aside dedicated time for employees to work on creative projects or host brainstorming sessions.

- Promote diversity and inclusion: Embrace diversity and work with colleagues who come from different backgrounds.

- Provide resources and support: Give employees the resources and support they need, such as technological resources, training and development opportunities, and mentorship programs.

- Encourage transparency: Share company goals and updates with employees and be open about decision-making processes.

- Recognize and reward collaboration: Thank employees for their contributions or showcase their work in company-wide meetings and consider implementing formal recognition programs.

- Foster a positive work environment: Create a positive and supportive atmosphere where employees feel happy and motivated to work.

- Encourage ongoing learning and development: Offer learning and development opportunities to help employees grow and improve their skills.

- Encourage collaboration with external partners: Consider working with external partners, such as suppliers, customers, and other organizations, to foster collaboration and bring in fresh perspectives.

- Encourage a growth mindset: Encourage employees to embrace challenges and see them as opportunities for learning and growth.

- Create a feedback-rich culture: Encourage employees to give and receive feedback in a constructive manner to help improve processes and encourage idea sharing.

- Use technology to facilitate collaboration: Use tools such as video conferencing and project management software to facilitate collaboration and communication among team members, especially if they are working remotely.

- Encourage a culture of trust: Build trust among employees by being honest, transparent, and supportive.

- Encourage risk-taking and experimentation: Encourage employees to take risks and try new approaches, even if they may not work out, as this can lead to new ideas and innovations.

- Encourage work-life balance: Help employees achieve a healthy work-life balance, as this can lead to increased productivity and creativity.

- Encourage a culture of accountability: Hold employees accountable for their work and encourage them to hold themselves and their colleagues accountable as well.

- Encourage employee engagement: Foster a sense of ownership and encourage employees to take an active role in decision-making processes.

- Encourage cross-functional collaboration: Bring together employees from different departments or teams to work on projects and share ideas.

- Encourage a culture of continuous improvement: Encourage employees to continuously seek out ways to improve processes and increase efficiency.

"The Power of Collaboration"

Alice was a bright and ambitious young employee at a technology company. She had always been a strong individual contributor, but she had always struggled to work effectively with others. She preferred to work on her own, and she often found it difficult to listen to the ideas of her colleagues.

One day, Alice's manager sat her down for a performance review. "Alice, we've noticed that while you're a talented individual contributor, you struggle to collaborate with your team," her manager said. "In this company, we value teamwork and the ability to share ideas. If you can't learn to work effectively with your colleagues, it will be difficult for you to succeed here."

Alice was taken aback by this feedback. She had always thought that she was doing just fine on her own, but she realized that she had been missing out on the benefits of collaboration. She decided to make a change and started actively seeking out opportunities to work with her colleagues.

At first, it was difficult for Alice to adjust. She had to learn to listen to others and compromise on ideas. But as she worked with her team, she began to see the power of collaboration. They were able to come up with solutions and ideas that she never would have thought of on her own. And as she became more comfortable working with others, she started to enjoy the process.

Before long, Alice's team was one of the most successful and productive in the company. She realized that by embracing collaboration, she had not only improved her own performance, but she had also helped her team achieve great things. Alice learned that while individual contributors are important, it's the power of the team that truly makes a difference.

As Alice's team continued to thrive, she found herself taking on more and more leadership responsibilities. She learned how to facilitate meetings, encourage open communication, and foster a sense of teamwork among her colleagues.

But Alice didn't stop there. She also worked to create a culture of collaboration and idea sharing throughout the entire company. She implemented regular team meetings, encouraged open communication, and provided resources and support to help her colleagues succeed.

As a result of Alice's efforts, the company experienced a surge in productivity and innovation. Employees were more engaged and motivated, and the company's bottom line improved. Alice's manager was thrilled with the results and promoted her to lead the company's collaboration and innovation efforts.

Alice's story demonstrates the power of collaboration and the importance of creating a culture of openness and idea sharing in the workplace. By embracing teamwork and encouraging her colleagues to share their ideas, Alice was able to achieve great success and help her company thrive.

Recognizing and rewarding innovation

Strategies for recognizing and rewarding employees who come up with new ideas and contribute to the company.

Innovation is the lifeblood of any organization. It is what allows companies to stay competitive and stay ahead of the curve. But for innovation to thrive, it's important to recognize and reward employees who come up with new ideas and contribute to the company's culture of innovation. In this book, we will explore strategies for recognizing and rewarding employees for their creative thinking.

- Encourage a culture of innovation: Encourage employees to think creatively and come up with new ideas and provide the resources and support they need to make their ideas a reality.

- Provide resources and support: Give employees the resources and support they need, such as technological resources, training and development opportunities, and mentorship programs.

- Encourage risk-taking and experimentation: Create a safe and supportive environment where employees feel comfortable taking risks and experimenting with new ideas.

- Recognize and reward innovation: Thank employees for their contributions or showcase their work in company-wide meetings and consider implementing formal recognition programs.

- Offer learning and development opportunities: Encourage ongoing learning and development through training programs, workshops, conferences, and on-the-job learning opportunities.

- Encourage collaboration with external partners: Work with external partners, such as suppliers, customers, and other organizations, to bring in fresh perspectives and ideas.

- Encourage a growth mindset: Encourage employees to embrace challenges and see them as opportunities for learning and growth.

- Create a feedback-rich culture: Encourage employees to give and constructively receive feedback to help improve processes and encourage idea sharing.

- Use technology to facilitate innovation: Use tools such as video conferencing and project management software to facilitate collaboration and communication among team members, especially if they are working remotely.

- Encourage a culture of trust: Build trust among employees by being honest, transparent, and supportive.

- Encourage employee engagement: Foster a sense of ownership and encourage employees to take an active role in decision-making processes.

- Encourage cross-functional collaboration: Bring together employees from different departments or teams to work on projects and share ideas.

- Encourage a culture of continuous improvement: Encourage employees to continuously seek out ways to improve processes and increase efficiency.

- Foster a positive work environment: Create a positive and supportive atmosphere where employees feel happy and motivated to work.

- Recognize and reward team efforts: In addition to recognizing individual contributions, consider recognizing and rewarding teams for their innovative efforts.

- Encourage employee involvement in goal setting: Involve employees in the goal-setting process to give them a sense of ownership and encourage them to come up with new ideas.

- Provide opportunities for creative expression: Encourage employees to express their creativity through things like art, music, or writing to foster innovation.

- Encourage experimentation and failure: Encourage employees to experiment and take risks, even if they may not always work out. Embrace failure as a learning opportunity.

- Encourage a culture of open communication: Encourage open communication and dialogue among employees to foster the sharing of ideas.

- Encourage employees to seek out new experiences: Encourage employees to try new things and learn from new experiences, as this can help stimulate creative thinking and innovation.

"The Innovator's Reward"

Ansh was an ambitious young employee at a marketing firm. he had always been a creative thinker, and he was always coming up with new ideas for campaigns and projects. But unfortunately, his ideas were often overlooked or dismissed by his colleagues and superiors.

One day, Ansh came up with an idea for a new social media campaign that he was convinced would be a hit. he presented it to her team, but they were skeptical and didn't seem interested in pursuing it. Frustrated, Ansh decided to take matters into his own hands and implemented the campaign on his own.

To everyone's surprise, the campaign was a huge success. It generated a lot of buzzes and helped to drive significant traffic to the company's website. Ansh's manager was impressed by his initiative and creativity, and he decided to recognize his efforts with a special award at the company's annual meeting.

Ansh was thrilled to receive the award and be recognized for his innovative thinking. It was a validation of his hard work and a testament to the value of his ideas. he realized that by fostering a culture of innovation and recognizing and rewarding employees for their creative thinking, his company was able to achieve great things.

Ansh's success inspired his colleagues to start thinking more creatively and coming up with their ideas. The company's culture of innovation began to thrive, and they started to see an increase in productivity and innovation.

Ansh's manager was thrilled with the results and decided to implement a formal recognition program to acknowledge the efforts of innovative employees. He also made a point to encourage risk-taking and experimentation and provided resources and support to help employees bring their ideas to fruition.

As a result of these efforts, the company continued to grow and succeed. Employees were more engaged and motivated, and the company's bottom line continued to improve. Ansh's story demonstrates the importance of recognizing and rewarding innovation in the workplace, and the positive impact it can have on a company's success.

Encouraging continuous learning

How leaders can create a culture of continuous learning, where employees are encouraged to seek out new knowledge?

In today's fast-paced business world, it's more important than ever for employees to continuously learn and grow. But fostering a culture of continuous learning can be a challenge. In this book, we will explore strategies that leaders can use to create a culture of continuous learning in the workplace, where employees are encouraged to seek out new knowledge and skills that can help them generate innovative ideas.

- Encourage ongoing learning and development: Encourage ongoing learning and development by offering employees access to a variety of learning opportunities, such as training programs, workshops, and conferences. You can also provide opportunities for on-the-job learning, such as job shadowing or mentorship programs.

- Provide resources and support: For continuous learning to thrive, it's important to provide employees with the resources and support they need. This can include everything from books and online courses to software and other technological resources.

- Encourage a growth mindset: Encourage a growth mindset among employees by encouraging them to embrace challenges and see them as opportunities for learning and growth. This can help create a culture of continuous learning, as employees will be more likely to seek out new experiences and knowledge.

- Encourage collaboration and idea-sharing: Encourage

collaboration and idea-sharing among employees to foster a culture of continuous learning. This can be as simple as encouraging employees to share their knowledge and expertise with their colleagues or hosting team brainstorming sessions.

- Encourage employees to take on new challenges: Encourage employees to take on new challenges and try new things. This can help stimulate creative thinking and encourage continuous learning.

- Encourage self-directed learning: Encourage employees to take an active role in their learning by encouraging self-directed learning. This can include things like setting learning goals, seeking out new resources and opportunities and taking on independent projects.

- Encourage a culture of continuous improvement: Encourage a culture of continuous improvement by encouraging employees to continuously seek out ways to improve processes and increase efficiency. This can help create a culture of continuous learning, as employees will be more likely to seek out new knowledge and skills to improve their work.

- Encourage a culture of openness and transparency: Encourage a culture of openness and transparency by being open and transparent with your employees. This can help create a culture

- Encourage employees to seek out new experiences: Encourage employees to seek out new experiences, such as traveling to new places or trying new hobbies, as this can help stimulate creative thinking and encourage continuous learning.

- Encourage employee engagement: Encourage employee engagement by involving employees in decision-making processes and giving them a sense of ownership in their work. This can help create a culture of continuous learning, as employees will be more likely to seek out new knowledge and skills to improve their work.

- Use technology to facilitate continuous learning: Use technology to facilitate continuous learning by providing employees with access to online resources, such as e-books and online courses, and by using tools such as video conferencing and project management software to facilitate collaboration and communication.

- Encourage cross-functional collaboration: Encourage cross-functional collaboration by bringing together employees from different departments or teams to work on projects and share ideas. This can help create a culture of continuous learning, as employees will be exposed to new perspectives and knowledge.

- Encourage a culture of mentorship: Encourage a culture of mentorship by implementing mentorship programs or encouraging experienced employees to mentor their colleagues. This can help create a culture of continuous learning, as employees will have the opportunity to learn from their more experienced colleagues.

- Encourage employee involvement in goal setting: Encourage employee involvement in goal setting by involving employees in the goal-setting process and giving them a sense of ownership in their work. This can help create a culture of continuous learning, as employees will be more likely to seek out new knowledge and skills to achieve their goals.

- Encourage employees to seek feedback: Encourage employees to seek feedback from their colleagues, superiors, and customers to improve their work and continuously learn.

- Encourage employees to take on leadership roles: Encourage employees to take on leadership roles, such as leading teams or projects, as this can help them develop new skills and encourage continuous learning.

- Encourage employees to seek out new job opportunities: Encourage employees to seek out new job opportunities, such as taking on new responsibilities or transitioning to a new role within the company, as this can help them develop new skills and encourage continuous learning.

- Encourage employees to seek out professional development opportunities: Encourage employees to seek out professional development opportunities, such as attending conferences or workshops, to continuously learn and grow.

- Encourage a culture of creativity: Encourage a culture of creativity by providing opportunities for employees to express their creativity and encourage them to think outside the box. This can help stimulate continuous learning, as employees will be more likely to seek out new knowledge and ideas.

- Encourage employees to share their knowledge and expertise: Encourage employees to share their knowledge and expertise with their colleagues by hosting knowledge-sharing sessions or encouraging employees to write articles or give presentations. This can help create a culture of continuous learning, as employees will be exposed to new perspectives and ideas.

"The Lifelong Learner"

Ayushman was an ambitious young employee at a tech company. he had always been curious and eager to learn, and he was always seeking out new knowledge and skills. But at his previous job, he had felt stuck and unable to grow. he was excited to join his new company because it had a reputation for fostering a culture of continuous learning.

As soon as Ayushman started at the company, he noticed a difference. Her manager encouraged him to take on new challenges and try new things and provided him with the resources and support he needed to learn and grow. Ayushman was thrilled to be allowed to learn and grow, and he took full advantage of it.

he attended conferences and workshops, took online courses, and sought out mentorship opportunities. he also made a point to collaborate with his colleagues and share his knowledge and expertise with them. Ayushman's manager was impressed with his dedication to continuous learning, and he recognized his efforts with a special award at the company's annual meeting.

Ayushman was proud of her accomplishment, but he knew that his learning journey was far from over. he was committed to being a lifelong learner and to help create a culture of continuous learning at his company. he knew that by fostering a culture of continuous learning, his company would be able to attract and retain top talent and stay ahead of the curve in an ever-changing industry.

Ayushman's commitment to continuous learning paid off in other ways as well. he developed a reputation as a knowledgeable and skilled employee, and he was frequently sought out by her colleagues for his expertise. he also found that her newfound knowledge and skills helped him to generate innovative ideas and contribute to the success of his team.

As the company grew and evolved, Ayushman continued to learn and grow with it. he took on new responsibilities and transitioned to new roles within the company, always looking for ways to challenge himself and improve. he was grateful to work for a company that valued continuous learning and recognized the importance of investing in its employees.

Ayushman's story demonstrates the positive impact that a culture of continuous learning can have on both individuals and organizations. By fostering a culture of continuous learning, leaders can help employees grow, stay engaged and motivated, and generate innovative ideas that can drive the success of the company.

EIGHT

Innovation and Customer Needs

How to use customer insights and feedback to drive innovation and create products or services that meet customer needs?

Innovation is essential for businesses to stay competitive and relevant, and understanding customer needs is a key part of the innovation process. By using customer insights and feedback to drive innovation, businesses can create products or services that meet the needs and preferences of their target market.

One way that businesses can use customer insights and feedback to drive innovation is by incorporating customer feedback into the innovation process. This involves gathering feedback from customers at various stages of the product development process and using that feedback to inform the design of new products or services. This can help businesses to identify unmet customer needs and create solutions that address those needs.

Another way that businesses can use customer insights and feedback to drive innovation is by involving customers in the innovation process through co-creation workshops or customer advisory boards. This involves working directly with customers to develop new ideas and gather feedback on prototypes. By involving customers in the innovation process, businesses can ensure that they are creating products or services that meet the needs and preferences of their target market.

Using customer insights and feedback to drive innovation can also involve testing new ideas with customers. This involves gathering feedback on prototypes and early versions of new products or services to identify any problems or areas for improvement. By testing new ideas with customers, businesses can ensure that they are developing products or services that meet the needs and preferences of their target market.

Overall, using customer insights and feedback to drive innovation is a key part of the innovation process. By incorporating customer feedback into the innovation process, involving customers in the innovation process, and testing new ideas with customers, businesses can create products or services that meet the needs and preferences of their target market.

Gathering customer insights

Techniques for gathering customer insights and feedback, such as customer interviews, surveys, and focus groups.

Understanding your customers is crucial for any business. By gathering customer insights and feedback, you can gain valuable insights into what your customers need and want and use this information to improve your products and services. In this book, we will explore techniques for gathering customer insights, including customer interviews, surveys, and focus groups.

- Conduct customer interviews to ask open-ended questions and get in-depth responses: Customer interviews involve talking to individual customers to ask open-ended questions and gather in-depth feedback.

- Use surveys to gather feedback on specific products or services or to get a general understanding of customer needs and preferences: Surveys allow you to gather feedback from a larger group of customers through the use of online tools or in-person or phone interviews.

- Host focus groups to gather insights and feedback from a group of customers: Focus groups involve bringing together a group of customers to discuss and provide feedback on specific topics related to your business.

- Monitor and review online reviews and ratings to get a sense of what customers are saying about your business: Online reviews and ratings provide insights into customer experiences with your products or services and can be found on websites such as Yelp or Amazon.

- Use social media monitoring to gather customer insights and feedback: Social media monitoring involves tracking and analysing what customers are saying about your business on social media platforms such as Twitter or Facebook.

- Include customer feedback forms on your website or in product packaging: Customer feedback forms can be included on your website or in product packaging to allow customers to provide feedback on their experiences.

- Conduct user testing to gather insights and feedback on usability and user experience: User testing involves having customers test your products or services to gather insights and feedback on usability and user experience.

- Use customer satisfaction surveys to measure customer satisfaction with your products or services: Customer satisfaction surveys measure how satisfied customers are with your products or services.

- Implement customer loyalty programs to gather insights and feedback from your most loyal customers: Customer loyalty programs reward and incentivize customers to share their thoughts and experiences with your business.

- Host customer focus groups to gather insights and feedback from a group of customers: Customer focus groups involve bringing together a group of customers to discuss and provide feedback on specific topics related to your business.

- Use customer journey mapping to understand the experiences and needs of your customers at different stages of their relationship with your business.: Customer journey mapping involves understanding the experiences and needs of customers at different stages of their relationship with your business.

- Gather feedback from customer service interactions, such as phone calls or email exchanges: Gathering feedback from customer service interactions, such as phone calls or email exchanges, can provide valuable insights into customer experiences and needs.

- Conduct usability testing to gather insights and feedback on the ease of use of your products or services: Usability testing involves testing the ease of use of your products or services to gather insights and feedback.

- Use A/B testing to gather insights and feedback on different versions of a product or service: A/B testing involves testing different versions of a product or service to gather insights and feedback on which version is preferred by customers.

- Utilize customer data analytics to understand customer behaviour and preferences: Utilizing customer data analytics involves analysing customer data to understand customer behaviour and preferences.

"The Voice of the Customer"

As the CEO of a successful software company, Jack always knew the importance of understanding his customers. But as the company grew, he found it increasingly difficult to gather insights and feedback directly from his customers. That's when he decided to hire a customer insights specialist, Ayushman.

Ayushman was a skilled researcher, with a background in market research and customer insights. He was tasked with gathering insights and feedback from the company's customers, through a variety of methods including surveys, focus groups, and customer interviews.

Jack was amazed at the wealth of information Ayushman was able to gather from the company's customers. He was able to identify areas where the company could improve, as well as new products and features that customer were interested in. Jack was grateful for Ayushman's insights, and he made sure to incorporate his feedback into the company's product development and customer service strategies.

Thanks to Ayushman's efforts, the company was able to better understand and meet the needs of its customers. As a result, customer satisfaction and loyalty increased, and the company saw a significant boost in sales. Jack knew that listening to the voice of the customer was crucial to the success of his business, and he made sure to continue gathering customer insights on an ongoing basis.

As Ayushman continued to gather customer insights, he became an invaluable resource for the company. He was able to identify trends and patterns in customer feedback, and he was able to provide valuable recommendations for how the company could improve its products and services.

One of Ayushman's biggest successes was his work on a customer loyalty program. He was able to gather insights from the company's most loyal customers, and he was able to design a program that offered meaningful rewards and incentives. The loyalty program was a huge success, and it helped to increase customer retention and loyalty.

Ayushman's work on the loyalty program caught the attention of other companies, and he was soon in high demand as a consultant. But he was committed to his role at Jack's software company, and he continued to work with them to gather customer insights and drive business success.

Jack was grateful to have Ayushman on his team, and he knew that his work was a key factor in the company's continued growth and success. He made sure to recognize and reward his efforts, and he encouraged other companies to follow his lead and prioritize gathering customer insights.

Analyzing customer data

Strategies for using data analytics tools to uncover insights about customer needs and preferences.

Customer data analytics is a powerful tool for businesses looking to better understand their customers and improve their products and services. By collecting and analyzing data from a variety of sources, businesses can uncover valuable insights into customer needs and preferences and use this information to inform their decision-making processes. Here are strategies for using data analytics tools to analyze customer data:

- Identify the business objectives for your customer data analysis. This will help guide your data collection and analysis efforts.

- Collect and organize customer data from a variety of sources, including customer surveys, social media, website analytics, and sales data.

- Clean and prepare the data for analysis, including checking for errors and missing values.

- Use data visualization tools to get a sense of the overall patterns and trends in the data.

- Segment the data by various criteria, such as demographic characteristics, purchase history, and behavior patterns, to get a more detailed understanding of customer needs and preferences.

- Use statistical analysis techniques, such as regression analysis and chi-square tests, to identify relationships and patterns in the data.

- Use machine learning algorithms to uncover hidden insights and predict future customer behavior.

- Use text analysis tools to analyze customer feedback and comments and identify common themes and sentiments.

- Use A/B testing to compare different versions of marketing campaigns and website designs to see which ones are most effective.

- Use customer journey mapping to understand the different touchpoints and interactions customers have with your brand and identify areas for improvement.

- Analyze customer lifetime value (CLV) to understand the value of different customer segments and identify opportunities to increase customer retention.

- Use social media analytics tools to understand how customers are interacting with your brand on social media platforms.

- Use customer feedback and ratings to identify areas of your product or service that are particularly important to customers.

- Use customer segmentation to create targeted marketing campaigns and personalized customer experiences.

- Use predictive analytics to identify potential churn risks and take proactive steps to prevent customer defection.

- Analyze customer behavior on your website or app to

identify areas for improvement and optimize the user experience.

- Use customer analytics to inform product development and design decisions.

- Use customer analytics to identify opportunities for cross-selling and upselling.

- Use customer analytics to inform your sales and customer service strategies, such as identifying high-value customers or identifying common customer pain points.

- Regularly review and update your customer data analysis strategies to ensure that you are staying up to date with the latest trends and techniques.

"Data Analytics Helps ABC Boutique Thrive."

A small online retail store, called "ABC Boutique," was struggling to attract and retain customers. The owner, Maria, knew she needed to better understand her customers to improve her business, but wasn't sure where to start.

One day, Maria attended a workshop on data analytics for small businesses and learned about the various strategies she could use to analyze customer data. She became particularly interested in customer segmentation, which involves dividing customers into groups based on shared characteristics or behaviors.

Maria decided to give it a try. She collected data on her customers' demographics, purchase history, and online behavior, and used a data visualization tool to identify trends and patterns. She discovered that her customers fell into three main segments: young professionals, busy moms, and budget-conscious students.

Using this information, Maria was able to create targeted marketing campaigns and personalized product recommendations for each customer segment. She also used customer feedback and ratings to improve the products and services offered in her store.

As a result of her efforts, ABC Boutique saw a significant increase in customer retention and sales. Maria was thrilled with the results and knew that she had data analytics to thank for helping turn her business around.

Maria's success with data analytics inspired her to dig even deeper into her customer data. She used machine learning algorithms to predict future customer behavior and identify potential churn risks. She also used customer journey mapping to understand the different touchpoints and interactions customers had with her brand and used this information to optimize the customer experience.

In addition, Maria used customer lifetime value (CLV) analysis to understand the value of different customer segments and identify opportunities to increase customer retention. She discovered that her high-value customers, who made up a small percentage of her customer base, were responsible for a significant portion of her sales. She focused on providing excellent customer service and targeted promotions to these valuable customers, which helped to further increase her sales.

Overall, Maria's use of data analytics helped her to gain a deep understanding of her customers and make informed business decisions that improved her bottom line. She knew that she needed to continue to analyze her customer data regularly to stay ahead of the competition and meet the evolving needs of her customers.

Incorporating customer feedback into the innovation process

Tips for using customer feedback to inform the development of new products and services.

Incorporating customer feedback into the innovation process is essential for businesses that want to create products and services that truly meet the needs and preferences of their customers. By actively seeking and gathering customer feedback, businesses can gain valuable insights into what their customers want and use this information to inform their innovation efforts. Here are tips for using customer feedback to inform the development of new products and services:

- Make it easy for customers to provide feedback, by offering multiple channels such as online surveys, social media, and customer service hotlines.

- Regularly solicit customer feedback, both formally through surveys and informally through casual conversations and interactions.

- Encourage open and honest feedback by making it clear that you value customer input and are committed to using it to improve your products and services.

- Analyze customer feedback using tools such as text analysis and sentiment analysis to identify common themes and sentiments.

- Use customer feedback to inform the development of new products and features, by prioritizing requests and ideas that are most frequently mentioned by customers.

- Use customer feedback to identify areas of your current products and services that need improvement and implement changes to address these issues.

- Involve customers in the innovation process by inviting them to participate in focus groups, beta testing, and other research and development activities.

- Use customer feedback to inform your marketing efforts, by identifying key messages and features that are most important to customers.

- Use customer feedback to inform your sales and customer service strategies, by identifying common customer pain points and areas of concern.

- Use customer feedback to inform your pricing and pricing strategies, by understanding what customers are willing to pay for and what they consider to be good value.

- Use customer feedback to identify opportunities for cross-selling and upselling, by understanding what complementary products or services customers are interested in.

- Use customer feedback to inform your product packaging and design decisions, by understanding what features and aesthetics are most appealing to customers.

- Use customer feedback to inform your product positioning and branding, by understanding what values and qualities customers associate with your brand.

- Use customer feedback to inform your distribution and fulfillment strategies, by understanding what delivery options and convenience factors are most important to customers.

- Use customer feedback to inform your customer experience strategies, by understanding what factors contribute to a positive customer experience.

- Use customer feedback to inform your social media and content marketing strategies, by understanding what topics and formats are most engaging to customers.

- Use customer feedback to inform your business model and value proposition, by understanding what customers value most about your products and services.

- Use customer feedback to inform your competitive analysis, by understanding how customers perceive your competitors and how you can differentiate yourself.

- Use customer feedback to inform your sustainability and corporate responsibility efforts, by understanding what environmental and social issues are most important to customers.

- Regularly review and update your customer feedback processes to ensure that you are continuously gathering and incorporating customer insights into your innovation efforts.

"Customer-Centric Innovation Boosts Business for Kate's Bakery"

Kate owned a small bakery that was struggling to stand out in a competitive market. She knew she needed to innovate to attract and retain customers but wasn't sure where to start.

One day, Kate attended a workshop on customer-centric innovation and learned about the importance of incorporating customer feedback into the innovation process. She realized that she had been so focused on running the day-to-day operations of her bakery that she hadn't tried to actively gather customer feedback.

Determined to turn things around, Kate implemented several changes to her business. She made it easy for customers to provide feedback, by offering online surveys and a suggestion box at the counter. She also made a point to regularly engage with customers and ask for their opinions on her products and services.

Kate was surprised by the amount of valuable feedback she received. Customers had a lot of ideas for new products and flavors, as well as suggestions for improving the customer experience at the bakery. Kate used this feedback to inform the development of new products and make changes to her existing offerings.

Kate's efforts paid off. By actively seeking and incorporating customer feedback, she was able to create a more engaging and satisfying customer experience, which helped to drive sales and increase customer loyalty. Kate knew that she needed to continue to gather and analyze customer feedback to stay ahead of the competition and meet the evolving needs of her customers.

Kate's bakery became known for its innovative products and excellent customer service, and she began to see an increase in foot traffic and sales. She used customer feedback to inform her marketing efforts, by highlighting the most popular products and features that customers had requested. She also used customer feedback to inform her pricing and pricing strategies, by understanding what customers were willing to pay for and what they considered to be good value.

Kate's bakery became a go-to destination for people looking for high-quality baked goods and an enjoyable customer experience. She received many positive reviews and recommendations from satisfied customers, which helped to further increase her sales and reputation.

In addition to using customer feedback to inform her product and service offerings, Kate also used it to inform her business model and value proposition. She learned that many of her customers valued the convenience and flexibility of online ordering, so she implemented an online ordering system and offered delivery options. She also learned that customers appreciated her commitment to using high-quality, locally sourced ingredients, so she emphasized this in her branding and marketing efforts.

Overall, Kate's commitment to gathering and incorporating customer feedback into her innovation process helped her to create a thriving and successful bakery. She knew that she needed to continue to listen to her customers and adapt to their changing needs in order to remain competitive and grow her business.

Designing for customer needs

Techniques for designing products and services that meet customer needs and solve customer problems.

Designing products and services that meet customer needs and solve customer problems is essential for businesses that want to create products and services that are valued by their customers. By taking a customer-centric approach to design, businesses can create products and services that are tailored to the needs and preferences of their target audience. Here are techniques for designing for customer needs:

- Understand your target audience and their needs, by conducting market research and gathering customer feedback.

- Identify customer problems and pain points, and design solutions that address these issues.

- Create customer personas to represent different segments of your target audience and use these to guide design decisions.

- Use design thinking techniques, such as empathy mapping and prototyping, to understand customer needs and create solutions.

- Involve customers in the design process, by gathering feedback and input during the design process.

- Use usability testing to ensure that your designs are intuitive and easy to use.

- Use A/B testing to compare different design options and

identify the most effective ones.

- Use customer journey mapping to understand the different touchpoints and interactions customers have with your products and services, and design for a seamless customer experience.

- Design for scalability and adaptability, by creating products and services that can be easily modified or updated to meet changing customer needs.

- Use customer feedback and ratings to identify areas of your products and services that need improvement and incorporate these changes into your designs.

- Consider sustainability and corporate responsibility in your design decisions, by creating products and services that have minimal environmental impact and promote social good.

- Design for accessibility, by creating products and services that can be used by people with different abilities and needs.

- Use data analytics and customer insights to inform your design decisions, by understanding what features and attributes are most important to customers.

- Consider the customer's entire experience with your product or service, including the packaging, instructions, and customer support, and design for an overall positive experience.

- Use customer feedback to identify opportunities for new products and services, and design these to meet customer needs.

- Use customer feedback to inform your branding and marketing efforts, by understanding what values and qualities customers associate with your brand.

- Design for customer convenience, by creating products and services that are easy to use and access.

- Design for customer value, by creating products and services that provide value for money.

- Consider the customer's emotional needs and design for positive emotions and experiences.

- Regularly review and update your design processes to ensure that you are continuously incorporating customer needs and feedback into your designs.

"Designing for Customer Needs Propels TechSolutions to Success"

A small software company, called "TechSolutions," was struggling to attract and retain customers. The owner, John, knew that he needed to create better products and services, but wasn't sure where to start.

One day, John attended a workshop on customer-centric design and learned about the importance of understanding and meeting customer needs. He realized that he had been so focused on creating products that he thought were cool and innovative, that he hadn't paid enough attention to what his customers actually wanted.

Determined to turn things around, John implemented a number of changes to his business. He gathered customer feedback and used it to inform the development of new products and features. He also involved customers in the design process, by gathering input and feedback during the design process.

John's efforts paid off. By designing products and services that were tailored to the needs and preferences of his customers, he was able to create a more engaging and satisfying customer experience.

As a result of his efforts, TechSolutions saw a significant increase in customer retention and sales. John's products were now known for their reliability, ease of use, and value for money, and he received many positive reviews and recommendations from satisfied customers.

In addition to using customer feedback to inform his product design, John also used it to inform his branding and marketing efforts. He learned that his customers valued the simplicity and clarity of his branding, so he made a point to emphasize these qualities in his marketing materials. He also used customer feedback to inform his pricing and pricing strategies, by understanding what customers were willing to pay for and what they considered to be good value.

Overall, John's commitment to designing for customer needs helped him to create a thriving and successful software company. He knew that he needed to continue to listen to his customers and adapt to their changing needs in order to remain competitive and grow his business.

Co-creation with customers

Strategies for involving customers in the innovation process, such as through co-creation workshops.

Involving customers in the innovation process can be a powerful way for businesses to create products and services that truly meet the needs and preferences of their target audience. By co-creating with customers, businesses can gain valuable insights and ideas that can inform their innovation efforts. Here are strategies for co-creation with customers:

- Identify key customer segments to involve in the co-creation process, based on their needs, preferences, and level of influence.

- Use various methods to gather customer input and ideas, such as online surveys, focus groups, and customer advisory boards.

- Use design thinking techniques, such as empathy mapping and prototyping, to understand customer needs and co-create solutions.

- Invite customers to participate in co-creation workshops, where they can collaborate with your team to generate and refine ideas.

- Use customer feedback and ratings to identify areas of your products and services that need improvement and involve customers in the process of finding solutions.

- Use customer journey mapping to understand the different touchpoints and interactions customers have with your products and services and involve customers in optimizing the customer experience.

- Use customer insights to inform your product development and design decisions, by understanding what features and attributes are most important to customers.

- Use customer insights to inform your marketing efforts, by understanding what messages and features are most compelling to customers.

- Use customer insights to inform your branding and positioning, by understanding what values and qualities customers associate with your brand.

- Use customer insights to inform your pricing and pricing strategies, by understanding what customers are willing to pay for and what they consider to be good value.

- Use customer insights to identify opportunities for new products and services and involve customers in the development process.

- Use customer insights to inform your sustainability and corporate responsibility efforts, by understanding what environmental and social issues are most important to customers.

- Use customer insights to inform your customer experience strategies, by understanding what factors contribute to a positive customer experience.

- Use customer insights to inform your business model and value proposition, by understanding what customers value most about your products and services.

- Involve customers in the testing and validation of new products and features, by inviting them to participate in beta testing or focus groups.

- Use customer insights to inform your competitive analysis, by understanding how customers perceive your competitors and how you can differentiate yourself.

- Use customer insights to inform your distribution and fulfilment strategies, by understanding what delivery options and convenience factors are most important to customers.

- Use customer insights to inform your social media and content marketing efforts, by understanding what topics and formats are most engaging to customers.

- Use customer insights to inform your customer service strategies, by understanding what common customer pain points and areas of concern need to be addressed.

- Regularly review and update your co-creation processes to ensure that you are continuously involving customers in your innovation efforts.

"Co-Creation Brings Playtime Toys Back to Life"

A small toy company, called "Playtime Toys," was struggling to keep up with the competition. The owner, Sarah, knew that she needed to create innovative products that would appeal to children and parents, but wasn't sure where to start.

One day, Sarah attended a workshop on co-creation and learned about the benefits of involving customers in the innovation process. She realized that she had been so focused on her own ideas and assumptions about what kids wanted, that she hadn't tried to actively gather customer insights.

Determined to turn things around, Sarah implemented a number of changes to her business. She invited children and parents to participate in co-creation workshops, where they could collaborate with her team to generate and refine ideas for new toys. She also set up a customer advisory board, made up of parents and children, to provide ongoing feedback and insights.

Sarah was surprised by the amount of valuable feedback she received. Children and parents had a lot of ideas for new toys and features, as well as suggestions for improving the customer experience at Playtime Toys. Sarah used this feedback to inform the development of new products and make changes to her existing offerings.

Testing new ideas with customers

Techniques for gathering feedback from customers on prototypes and early versions of new products and services.

Gathering feedback from customers on prototypes and early versions of new products and services is essential for businesses that want to create products and services that truly meet the needs and preferences of their target audience. By testing new ideas with customers, businesses can identify and address any issues or concerns before a product or service is fully launched. Here are techniques for testing new ideas with customers:

- Identify key customer segments to involve in the testing process, based on their needs, preferences, and level of influence.

- Use various methods to gather customer feedback on prototypes and early versions of new products and services, such as focus groups, online surveys, and one-on-one interviews.

- Use usability testing to ensure that prototypes and early versions of new products and services are intuitive and easy to use.

- Use A/B testing to compare different prototypes or versions of a product or service and identify the most effective ones.

- Invite customers to participate in beta testing, where they can test and provide feedback on new products and services.

- Use customer journey mapping to understand the different touchpoints and interactions customers have with your products and services and involve customers in testing and optimizing the customer experience.

- Use customer insights to inform your product development and design decisions, by understanding what features and attributes are most important to customers.

- Use customer insights to inform your marketing efforts, by understanding what messages and features are most compelling to customers.

- Use customer insights to inform your branding and positioning, by understanding what values and qualities customers associate with your brand.

- Use customer insights to inform your pricing and pricing strategies, by understanding what customers are willing to pay for and what they consider to be good value.

- Use customer insights to identify opportunities for new products and services and involve customers in the testing and validation process.

- Use customer insights to inform your sustainability and corporate responsibility efforts, by understanding what environmental and social issues are most important to customers.

- Use customer insights to inform your customer experience strategies, by understanding what factors contribute to a positive customer experience.

- Use customer insights to inform your business model and value proposition, by understanding what customers value most about your products and services.

- Use customer insights to inform your distribution and fulfillment strategies, by understanding what delivery options and convenience factors are most important to customers.

- Use customer insights to inform your social media and content marketing efforts, by understanding what topics and formats are most engaging to customers.

- Use customer insights to inform your customer service strategies, by understanding what common customer pain points and areas of concern need to be addressed.

- Regularly review and update your testing processes to ensure that you are continuously involving customers in the development of new products and services.

- Use customer feedback to identify and address any issues or concerns with prototypes or early versions of new products and services.

- Use customer feedback to refine and improve prototypes or early versions of new products and services, based on customer needs and preferences.

-

"Testing New Ideas with Customers Revives Stylish Threads"

A small fashion company, called "Stylish Threads," was struggling to stay relevant in a rapidly changing market. The owner, Rachel, knew that she needed to create new and innovative products, but wasn't sure where to start.

One day, Rachel attended a workshop on customer-centric innovation and learned about the importance of testing new ideas with customers. She realized that she had been so focused on her creative vision that she hadn't tried to gather feedback from her customers.

Determined to turn things around, Rachel implemented several changes to her business. She invited customers to participate in focus groups and one-on-one interviews, where they could provide feedback on prototypes and early versions of new products. She also set up an online survey to gather customer insights regularly.

Rachel was surprised by the amount of valuable feedback she received. Customers had a lot of ideas for new products and styles, as well as suggestions for improving the customer experience at Stylish Threads. Rachel used this feedback to inform the development of new products and make changes to her existing offerings.

Building customer loyalty through innovation

Strategies for using innovation to build customer loyalty and drive repeat business.

Using innovation to build customer loyalty and drive repeat business is crucial for businesses that want to create a strong and loyal customer base. By continuously introducing new and improved products and services, businesses can keep their customers engaged and satisfied. Here are strategies for building customer loyalty through innovation:

- Identify key customer segments to target with your innovation efforts, based on their needs, preferences, and level of influence.

- Use customer feedback and insights to inform your innovation efforts, by understanding what customers want and need.

- Use design thinking techniques, such as empathy mapping and prototyping, to understand customer needs and co-create solutions.

- Involve customers in the innovation process, by gathering feedback and input during the design process.

- Use usability testing to ensure that your innovations are intuitive and easy to use.

- Use A/B testing to compare different prototypes or versions of a product or service and identify the most effective ones.

- Invite customers to participate in beta testing, where they can test and provide feedback on new products and services.

- Use customer journey mapping to understand the different touchpoints and interactions customers have with your products and services and involve customers in optimizing the customer experience.

- Use customer insights to inform your product development and design decisions, by understanding what features and attributes are most important to customers.

- Use customer insights to inform your marketing efforts, by understanding what messages and features are most compelling to customers.

- Use customer insights to inform your branding and positioning, by understanding what values and qualities customers associate with your brand.

- Use customer insights to inform your pricing and pricing strategies, by understanding what customers are willing to pay for and what they consider to be good value.

- Use customer insights to identify opportunities for new products and services and involve customers in the development process.

- Use customer insights to inform your sustainability and corporate responsibility efforts, by understanding what environmental and social issues are most important to customers.

- Use customer insights to inform your customer experience strategies, by understanding what factors contribute to a positive customer experience.

- Use customer insights to inform your business model and value proposition, by understanding what customers value most about your products and services.

- Use customer insights to inform your distribution and fulfilment strategies, by understanding what delivery options and convenience factors are most important to customers.

- Use customer insights to inform your social media and content marketing efforts, by understanding what topics and formats are most engaging to customers.

- Use customer insights to inform your customer service strategies, by understanding what common customer pain points and areas of concern need to be addressed.

- Regularly review and update your innovation processes to ensure that you are continuously involving customers in your efforts to build customer loyalty.

"Innovation Leads to Loyalty at Living Spaces"

A small home decor company, called "Living Spaces," was struggling to stand out in a crowded market. The owner, Maria, knew that she needed to create innovative and unique products, but wasn't sure where to start.

One day, Maria attended a workshop on customer-centric innovation and learned about the importance of involving customers in the innovation process. She realized that she had been so focused on her own creative vision that she hadn't tried to gather feedback from her customers.

Determined to turn things around, Maria implemented a number of changes to her business. She invited customers to participate in focus groups and one-on-one interviews, where they could provide feedback on prototypes and early versions of new products. She also set up an online survey to gather customer insights on a regular basis.

Maria things around, Maria began to see significant changes in her business. Customers were excited about the new and innovative products that she was introducing, and many of them became loyal customers who returned to Living Spaces time and time again. Maria's efforts to build customer loyalty through innovation paid off, and she was able to not only stay relevant in the market, but also thrive.

Measuring customer satisfaction

Techniques for tracking customer satisfaction with new products and services and using feedback to improve them.

Tracking customer satisfaction with new products and services and using feedback to improve them is crucial for businesses that want to create products and services that truly meet the needs and preferences of their target audience. By measuring customer satisfaction, businesses can identify and address any issues or concerns, and ensure that their products and services are continuously improving. Here are techniques for measuring customer satisfaction:

- Identify key customer segments to target with your customer satisfaction efforts, based on their needs, preferences, and level of influence.

- Use various methods to gather customer feedback on new products and services, such as focus groups, online surveys, and one-on-one interviews.

- Use usability testing to ensure that new products and services are intuitive and easy to use.

- Use A/B testing to compare different versions of a product or service and identify the most effective ones.

- Invite customers to participate in beta testing, where they can test and provide feedback on new products and services.

- Use customer journey mapping to understand the different touchpoints and interactions customers have with your products and services and involve customers in optimizing the customer experience.

- Use customer insights to inform your product development and design decisions, by understanding what features and attributes are most important to customers.

- Use customer insights to inform your marketing efforts, by understanding what messages and features are most compelling to customers.

- Use customer insights to inform your branding and positioning, by understanding what values and qualities customers associate with your brand.

- Use customer insights to inform your pricing and pricing strategies, by understanding what customers are willing to pay for and what they consider to be good value.

- Use customer insights to identify opportunities for new products and services and involve customers in the development process.

- Use customer insights to inform your sustainability and corporate responsibility efforts, by understanding what environmental and social issues are most important to customers.

- Use customer insights to inform your customer experience strategies, by understanding what factors contribute to a positive customer experience.

- Use customer insights to inform your business model and value proposition, by understanding what customers value most about your products and services.

- Use customer insights to inform your distribution and fulfilment strategies, by understanding what delivery options and convenience factors are most important to customers.

- Use customer insights to inform your social media and content marketing efforts, by understanding what topics and formats are most engaging to customers.

- Use customer insights to inform your customer service strategies, by understanding what common customer pain points and areas of concern need to be addressed.

- Regularly review and update your customer satisfaction processes to ensure that you are continuously gathering and analysing customer feedback.

- Use customer satisfaction data to identify and address any issues or concerns with new products and services.

- Use customer satisfaction data to refine and improve new products and services, based on customer needs and preferences.

"Measuring Customer Satisfaction Revives Tech Solutions"

A small software company, called "Tech Solutions," was struggling to keep up with the fast-paced and competitive tech industry. The owner, Alex, knew that he needed to create innovative and high-quality products, but wasn't sure how to ensure that his products were meeting the needs and preferences of his customers.

One day, Alex attended a workshop on customer-centric innovation and learned about the importance of measuring customer satisfaction. He realized that he had been so focused on developing new products that he hadn't tried to gather feedback from his customers.

Determined to turn things around, Alex implemented a number of changes to his business. He invited customers to participate in focus groups and one-on-one interviews, where they could provide feedback on new products. He also set up an online survey to gather customer insights on a regular basis.

Alex was surprised by the amount of valuable feedback he received. Customers had a lot of suggestions for improving his products and the customer experience at Tech Solutions. Alex used this feedback to make changes to his products and improve the overall customer experience.

Bibliography

- *"The Innovator's Dilemma"* by **Clayton M. Christensen**
- *"Design Thinking: Integrating Innovation, Customer Experience, and Brand Value"* by **Tim Brown**
- *"The Art of Possibility"* by **Rosamund Stone Zander and Benjamin Zander**
- *"Lateral Thinking: Creativity Step by Step"* by **Edward de Bono**
- *"The Lean Startup"* by **Eric Ries**

About The Author

Rohan Shaw is the author of "A Book on Innovation and Creativity in the Business World, including Strategies for Generating New Ideas and Implementing Them Effectively." At the age of 17, Rohan has already demonstrated a strong interest in business and innovation and has compiled his insights and ideas into this comprehensive guide. Rohan isn't just an author, he's also an aspiring entrepreneur. In the near future, he plans to launch his own startup and make his mark on the business world.

Rohan believes in the importance of fostering a culture of innovation in the workplace and provides practical strategies for creating an environment that encourages employees to come up with new ideas and take risks. He also presents a variety of techniques for generating new ideas, as well as tools for evaluating and selecting the best ideas. Rohan's book is a valuable resource for anyone looking to boost creativity and innovation in their business or organization.

In addition to his work as an author, Rohan Shaw is also an avid learner and seeker of new knowledge. He believes in the importance of continuous learning and encourages others to embrace this mindset as well. Rohan is passionate about helping organizations and individuals tap into their creative potential and achieve success. His book is a testament to this passion, as it provides a wealth of practical advice and techniques for fostering creativity and innovation.

Rohan hopes that his book will inspire readers to think creatively, take risks, and pursue their ideas with determination and enthusiasm. He is confident that by following the strategies outlined in his book, anyone can create an environment that promotes innovation and drive their business or organization forward.

With "Innovation and Creativity in the Business World," Rohan is well on his way to achieving his goals and helping others do the same.

Don't miss out on this valuable resource – get your copy!

GLOSSARY

- **Adaptive leadership** - A leadership approach that focuses on the ability to adapt and respond to change, rather than following a fixed plan or agenda
- **Brainstorming** - A group problem-solving technique in which ideas are generated and discussed openly in a free-flowing manner
- **Collaboration** - The act of working together with others towards a common goal
- **Creative expression** - The act of expressing oneself creatively, through activities such as art, music, writing, or design
- **Creative problem-solving** - The process of coming up with innovative solutions to complex or challenging problems
- **Design thinking** - A creative approach to problem-solving that involves empathy, prototyping, and iteration
- **Empathy** - The ability to understand and share the feelings of others
- **Feasibility** - The likelihood that a project or idea can be successfully implemented
- **Innovation** - The process of introducing something new or different, or the result of such a process
- **Innovative thinking** - The ability to come up with new ideas and approaches to problems
- **Lateral thinking** - A creative problem-solving approach that involves looking at a problem from different angles and considering alternative solutions
- **SCAMPER** - A technique for generating new ideas by considering different ways to modify, combine, adapt, put to other uses, eliminate, rearrange, or reverse existing products, or ideas

- **Workplace culture** - The values, beliefs, and behaviors that shape the work environment and help people work together

www.ingramcontent.com/pod-product-compliance
Lightning Source LLC
Chambersburg PA
CBHW020638220526
45464CB00001B/197